r Richard Race, Roeham~~ ~ '~

EDUCATION POLICY AND RACIAL BIOPOLITICS IN MULTICULTURAL CITIES

Kalervo N. Gulson and P. Taylor Webb

First published in Great Britain in 2017 by

Policy Press
University of Bristol
1-9 Old Park Hill
Bristol
BS2 8BB
UK
t: +44 (0)117 954 5940
pp-info@bristol.ac.uk
www.policypress.co.uk

North America office:
Policy Press
c/o The University of Chicago Press
1427 East 60th Street
Chicago, IL 60637, USA
t: +1 773 702 7700
f: +1 773-702-9756
sales@press.uchicago.edu
www.press.uchicago.edu

British Library Cataloguing in Publication Data
A catalogue record for this book is available from the British Library

Library of Congress Cataloging-in-Publication Data
A catalog record for this book has been requested

ISBN 978-1-4473-2007-4 hardcover
ISBN 978-1-4473-3521-4 ePub
ISBN 978-1-4473-3522-1 Mobi
ISBN 978-1-4473-2008-1 ePdf

The right of Kalervo N. Gulson and P. Taylor Webb to be identified as authors of this work has been asserted by them in accordance with the Copyright, Designs and Patents Act 1988.

The statements and opinions contained within this publication are solely those of the authors and not of the University of Bristol or Policy Press. The University of Bristol and Policy Press disclaim responsibility for any injury to persons or property resulting from any material published in this publication.

Policy Press works to counter discrimination on grounds of gender, race, disability, age and sexuality.

Cover design by Policy Press
Front cover image: kindly supplied by Jeremy Laws

Contents

Notes on authors

Kalervo N. Gulson is Associate Professor in the Faculty of Arts and Social Sciences, University of New South Wales. His research is located across social, political and cultural geography, education policy studies, and science and technology studies. Work relevant to this book includes (1) conceptualising the role of space in policy studies; and (2) the spatial dimensions of racial and cultural relations, and education policy in cities. Recent publications in these areas include *Policy, geophilosophy and education* (Sense, 2015, with P. Taylor Webb) and *Education policy, space and the city: markets and the (in)visibility of race* (2011, Routledge).

P. Taylor Webb is Associate Professor in the Department of Educational Studies within the Faculty of Education at the University of British Columbia, Vancouver. His research is located across social and cultural theory, continental philosophy, education policy studies and post-qualitative methodologies. Recent publications relevant to this book include: *Policy, geophilosophy and education* (Sense, 2015, with K.N. Gulson), and *Teacher assemblage* (Sense, 2009).

Acknowledgements

We would like to thank Amy Metcalfe, Matthew Clarke, Terezia Zoric, Carl James, David Gillborn, Zeus Leonardo, Duncan McDuie-Ra, Deborah Youdell, Jessica Gerrard, Michael Dumas, Ee-Seul Yoon, William Pinar and countless others, for arguments and discussions in workshops, conferences, cafes and pubs. Any errors and claims remain ours alone.

We thank our friend and colleague Eva Bendix Petersen for challenging us to write a different kind of book about policy, race and cities. We hope we have done some justice to that challenge.

Thank you to all community members and Toronto District School Board trustees who talked with us about the establishment of the Africentric Alternative School, and about race and schooling in Toronto more generally.

Thank you to our commissioning editor at Policy Press, Isobel Bainton, for her patience over the past two years while we went through some trying times. We acknowledge the project funding from the Canadian Social Sciences and Humanities Research Council. This book would not have been possible without the exemplary and amazing work done by Dr Viviana Pitton as a research associate on the funded project.

As always, thanks to our families: Kim, Finn, Kobi and Aila; and Amy and Owen.

We have reworked the following papers in this book:

Gulson, K.N. and Webb, P.T. (2012) Education policy racialisations: Afrocentric schools, Islamic schools and the new enunciations of equity, *Journal of Education Policy*, 27, 6, 697–710

Gulson, K.N. and Webb, P.T. (2013) A raw, emotional thing: school choice, commodification and the racialised branding of Afrocentricity in Toronto, Canada, *Education Inquiry*, 4, 1, 805–25

Gulson, K.N. and Webb, P.T. (2016) Not just another alternative school: policy problematization, neoliberalism, and racial biopolitics, *Educational Policy*, 30, 1, 153–70.

Webb, P.T., Gulson, K.N. and Pitton, V. (2012) The neo-liberal policies of epimelia heautou: caring for the self in school markets, *Discourse: Studies in the Cultural Politics of Education*, 35, 1, 31–44

Webb, P.T. and Gulson, K.N. (2014) Faciality enactments, schools of recognition and policies of difference (in-itself), *Discourse: Studies in the Cultural Politics of Education*, 36, 4, 515–32

Foreword

We might start with Montravious Thomas, and how he lost his leg. In early September 2016, the 13-year-old Black boy was cited for disruptive behaviour at his home school, in Muscogee County, Georgia. School district administrators ordered him to spend four days at Edgewood Student Services Centre, an alternative school for children with behavioural difficulties. This was the first time that Montravious had ever been in trouble, and he did not have a history of violent outbursts or altercations.

On his first day at Edgewood, Montravious tried to leave the classroom to call his mother. A school behavioural specialist intervened, and ultimately body-slammed Montravious to the ground three times to prevent him from leaving the room. Montravious complained that his leg felt numb, and that he couldn't walk. School officials thought he was exaggerating about the extent of his pain. The same behavioural specialist then threw the boy over his shoulder and took him to the school bus, and Montravious was taken home.

But Montravious was not exaggerating. Later that night, his mother took him to the emergency room, and he was subsequently airlifted to a hospital in the nearby city of Atlanta. The internal injuries he sustained in the assault by the school official at Edgewood were severe. Doctors attempted several emergency surgeries to get blood flowing back to his limb. When these efforts failed, they told Montravious and his mother that the only choice left was to amputate his leg. His right leg.

In this text on critical policy theorising about Black-focused schooling, I start with Montravious Thomas because this child – and the act of violence committed against him – serve as meditations on Black education, and more specifically, on the role of social and education policies in either mitigating or exacerbating Black suffering in schools. In this specific case, Montravious was removed from his home school due to some violation of the school behavioural code. Yet, we know that Black children are more likely to be surveilled that any other racial(ised) group, and more likely to receive harsh disciplinary sanctions (Crenshaw, 2015; Ferguson, 2000; Ladson-Billings, 2011). The research suggests that Black parents and caregivers often experience frustration as they attempt to advocate for their own children in schools (Reynolds, Howard & Jones, 2013; Reynolds, 2015). We also know that Black teachers are more likely to have higher expectations of Black children and less likely to view them as suspect or damaged; yet, Black students have limited opportunities to experience learning with Black educators (Lindsay & Hart, 2017). And more broadly, scholars of Black education have documented that traditional school environments are often sites of Black social suffering and anti-Black terror (Dumas, 2014; Pabon, 2016; Wun, 2016).

Starting with Montravious Thomas brings into view a set of interconnected educational policy issues – school discipline, teacher hiring and retention, (mal)distribution of resources along racial lines, student achievement, culturally relevant and sustaining curriculum and pedagogy. We can see more clearly the connections between policy and everyday life and death, and move towards a more critical theorisation and explanation of Black education policy discourses and practices, in the public sphere and in Black cultural spaces.

This is what Kalervo Gulson and Taylor Webb describe here as 'starting in the middle'. In this approach, critical policy analysis and theorising proceeds from consideration of (seemingly) singular events, not to make a causal or inductive inference, but to make sense of relationships between several events, the social imagination of the 'problem', and the production of policy intended to respond to that 'problem'. It is not that events have meanings in themselves, but it is accounts of events, taken together, that promise to reveal how power works in the construction of the stories we tell ourselves and are told about policy, and then the effects of those constructions on policy deliberation, implementation, evaluation, and ongoing contestation. The 'middle', as I understand it, refuses a linear ordering of events, and thus opens up the temporal and spatial terrain to consider that policies do not have determined or bounded beginnings and ends. In this sense, then, I can choose to start with Montravious Thomas, knowing that this singular event in the US state of Georgia in 2016, is linked to the creation of the Africentric Alternative School in Toronto, Ontario, over the course of several decades, because both are connected to a more general yearning for a response to the problem of what Carter G. Woodson (1933) long ago described as 'the miseducation' of Black people. The 'middle', then, is not one singular location, but a space where a broad range of events, and accounts of these events, can be brought together for critical policy analysis and explanation.

Gulson and Webb focus on four important frames – or what they call 'preconditions' – through which to understand the creation of this Black-focused school: racial biopolitics; neoliberalism; the politics of recognition; and the city and its relationships to race and multiculturalism. As they explain, 'The becoming of the school was affected through this set of preconditions, and the combination with a few others. At different times, these preconditions mediated how people lived and, more importantly, which people lived. In other words, the preconditions ostensibly functioned to administer, influence and control the lives of different populations' (p. 21). So here, it becomes important to understand policy as a form of racial biopolitics and as a space in which neoliberal structures shape our subjectivities and desires; policy is also enacted through the recognition (or perhaps misrecognition) of racialised bodies, often in an effort to displace attention from the necessary redistribution of economic resources. And finally, Gulson and Webb argue, policy is a site in which we produce and enact visions of the city, and specifically for whom that city will exist in the future. They seem intrigued – perhaps more than I am – about the possibilities of a post-racial city, in which racial identities are given up in favour of new subjectivities that allow us to live cognizant of, but unencumbered by our history of racial terror. But whether a post-racial city, or one in which Black bodies and collective desires continue to pose a threat to neoliberal multiculturalism, what Gulson and Webb provide here is an understanding that the city matters, that the (racialised) city must always be a unit of analysis in the study of education politics.

The authors acknowledge that the frames (or preconditions) they have chosen are not exhaustive, but are among those that are often unexplored, obscured, missing. One of the primary aims of a decidedly critical education policy analysis is to attend to these silences in policy discourse, because these silences are most often the imposition of power. That is, what is left unsaid, what cannot be said, is that knowledge – policy knowledge – held by those violently placed at the margins. Normative education policy analysis is guided by the interests of nation-states, market forces, and publics that have the power to exploit, erase, and exact terror against those who are socially imagined as only on the receiving end of policy. It is not that these groups lack educational desires, or fail to participate in policy deliberation; rather, it is that they are not socially recognised as entitled to exercise agency in the city and in planning for the city. Thus, they are understood as the objects, rather than the subjects, of education policy. The questions that then get posed by researchers and by the public about the affordance and limitations of policy, about policy effects, about the 'problem' itself, reflect the interests of those in power, who fund research and/or hold political sway over policy priorities of governmental and educational leaders (Dumas & Anderson, 2014). For example, in much research and public discourse on school desegregation in the United States, the focus is on demonstrating the benefits of racial diversity in integrated schools. Although some attention is given to the positive effects of attending integrated schools for Black students and other students of colour, the primary aim is to demonstrate that white students will benefit from exposure to racially different others, both in terms of their education but also in terms of their ability to accumulate wealth in multicultural markets (Wells, et. al, 2008). In sharp contrast, most critical Black perspectives on school desegregation – those that emphasise the importance of the lives and experiences of Black children, families, and communities – are concerned with how integration might improve Black students' access to educational resources. This body of work balances possible social, emotional, and educational benefits of diversity with the costs: a curriculum which ignores or misrepresents Black history and life, teachers and peers with biases against Black people, loss of the school as a community-based institution (Bell, 2004; DuBois, 1935; Dumas, 2011, 2014; Walker, 1996). This critical policy research speaks into the silences imposed and reproduced in so much scholarship and public discourse.

Through the case study of the Black-focused alternative school, Gulson and Webb offer us a promising approach to the analysis of race in urban education policy. By exploring the imbrication of this one event and a broader set of preconditions within the spatial context of the city (and the nation-state), the authors are able to demonstrate how we make meaning of education policy, but also how education policy makes meaning of us. This is true in the public sense of 'us,' by which we may mean to refer to the polity, or some notion of the public sphere. But I am also interested in the possibility of critical policy analysis in refusing the public. And here, I read the Black desires in the creation of the Africentric Alternative School as imbued with a decided interest in other, counter-public futurities. Black futurities, in and outside of schools.

Which brings me back to Montravious Thomas. And the middle. Because there is no singular, totalising explanation for why a school official assaulted him, and damaged his right leg to the point that it could not be saved. There is also no singular policy or intervention that will prevent other young Black children from being subjected to suffering and terror in school and in the city. But it may be that an analysis that interrogates power in all its dispersed moments and spaces might have something meaningful to offer a politics that does the same.

Michael J. Dumas
University of California, Berkeley
April 2017

References

Bell, D. (2004) *Silent covenants: Brown v. Board of Education and the unfulfilled hopes for racial reform*, Oxford: Oxford University Press

Crenshaw, K. (2015) *Black girls matter: Pushed out, overpoliced and underprotected*, New York: African American Policy Forum

DuBois, W. B. (1935) Does the Negro need separate schools? *Journal of Negro Education*, 328–335

Dumas, M. J. (2011) A cultural political economy of school desegregation in Seattle, *Teachers College Record, 113*(4), 703–734

Dumas, M. J. (2014) 'Losing an arm': Schooling as a site of black suffering, *Race Ethnicity and Education, 17*(1), 1–29

Dumas, M., and Anderson, G. L. (2014) Qualitative research as policy knowledge: Framing policy problems and transforming education from the ground up, *Education policy analysis archives, 22*, 11

Ferguson, A. A. (2000) *Bad boys: Public schools in the making of Black masculinity*, Ann Arbor: University of Michigan

Ladson-Billings, G. (2011) Boyz to men? Teaching to restore Black boys' childhood, *Race, Ethnicity and Education, 14*(1), 7–15

Lindsay, C.A., and Hart, C.M.D. (2017) Exposure to same-race teachers and student disciplinary outcomes for Black students in North Carolina, *Educational Evaluation and Policy Analysis*. doi: 10.3102/0162373717693109

Pabon, A. J. M. (2016) In hindsight and now again: Black male teachers' recollections on the suffering of black male youth in US public schools, *Race Ethnicity and Education*, 1–15

Reynolds, R. E. (2015) We've been post-raced: An examination of negotiations between race, agency, and school structures black families experience within post-racial schools, *Teachers College Record, 117*(14), 148–170

Reynolds, R. E., Howard, T.C., and Jones, T.K. (2013) Is this what educators really want? Transforming the discourse on Black fathers and their participation in schools, *Race, Ethnicity and Education*, 1–19

Walker, V. S. (1996) *Their highest potential: An African American school community in the segregated South*, Columbia: University of North Carolina Press

Wells, A. S., Duran, J., and White, T. (2008) Refusing to leave desegregation behind: From graduates of racially diverse schools to the Supreme Court, *Teachers College Record, 110*(12), 2532–2570

Woodson, C. G. (1933) *The miseducation of the Negro*, Washington, DC: Associated Publishers

Wun, C. (2016) Against captivity: Black girls and school discipline policies in the afterlife of Slavery, *Educational policy, 30*(1), 171–196

Introduction: education policy and multicultural cities

> I'm not against specialized curricula, but having separate schools for blacks or other ethnic students is as offensive as white-only washrooms. I object to educational apartheid because it turns back the clock on civil rights ... Schools socialize us into becoming Canadians. They help us cross class and racial lines so we can head into the workplace. Separate schools with monocultural learning environments are antithetical to the principles on which our public school system is based: openness, integration, cohesion. How can you eliminate racism by segregating along racial lines? (Wong, 2011: np)

> Multiculturalism is the toxic gift that keeps on giving. (Lentin and Titley, 2011: 3)

This is a book about how a small Black-focused school came to be in a global, multicultural city. It is a story of the imbrications of education policy, markets, difference and race in the city.

In September 2009, just over 100 students entered the classrooms of the Africentric[1] Alternative School for the first time. A kindergarten to grade five school, later expanded to grade eight, the Africentric school opened as an elementary school-within-a-school at the existing Sheppard Public School in the northwest area of Toronto. It was the first Black-focused elementary school to be established by the Toronto District School Board (TDSB), a school district with 600 schools and close to 300,000 students, of whom 12%, or 31,800, students identified as Black (Yau et al, 2011). According to the school website: '[a] unique feature of the AAS [Africentric Alternative School] will be the integration of the diverse perspectives, experiences and histories of people of African descent into the provincial mandated curriculum' (AAS, 2011). The curricula approaches in the school broadly accord with the approaches of Black-focused schools in the United States of America, many of which were established in the first instance in the 1960s and 1970s, that draw on a transnational and diasporic set of Afrocentric knowledges and politics (Dei 1996; Dei and Kempf, 2013).

The Africentric Alternative School was one of four elementary schools that opened as part of the 'alternative schools' programme in September 2009, as part of a Toronto education policy framework that not only enabled choice, in allowing parents choose to send their children to existing alternative schools, but also allowed for the *establishment* of new schools by parents and other interested parties. There are more than 40 elementary and secondary alternative schools in Toronto (TDSB, 2012).

While the alternative schools have not always been seen as part of school choice, in the case of the Africentric Alternative School, it was positioned by the district as part of its suite of choice options. In January 2008, when the school was approved by the TDSB, the newly elected TDSB Chair John Campbell argued that he was not opposed to the idea of a Black-focused school. Rather, he saw it in economic terms 'as our customers are students and parents; our product is education. We have declining enrolment and we have a group of customers that is dissatisfied and not doing well, or some of them aren't doing well, and we have to figure out a way to address that' (Rushowy, 2008).

School choice in Canada is the legislative remit of the provinces, and then reconfigured and enacted at school board levels (Davies, 2004). Toronto, like many other cities, has a local education quasi-market, with a combination of state control and market mechanisms (Taylor, 2009). While a quasi-market valorises the figure of the 'consumer-parent', there is less emphasis on the idea of the 'producer-parent' who can play a role in establishing schools. This is a particular formation of choice policy that permits the creation of separate, publicly funded educational spaces (Wells et al, 1999). However, as we will explore in this book, not all educational spaces are created equal. Afrocentric schools had been debated as a schooling option for the Black community since the 1970s, and Afrocentric-focused schools existed in the eastern provinces of Nova Scotia and New Brunswick for a while. Nevertheless, when the Africentric Alternative School was proposed in the 21st century it was enmeshed in controversy, even though alternative schools had been a part of the Toronto public education landscape for over 30 years.

It is the idea of some choices as being more equal than others that, for us, leads to an interest in the imbrications of space and the city, race and difference, and choice and policy. While the work that underpins this book was initially to be drawn from a funded research project investigating connections between curriculum, identity and policy, we were not able to gain access to the school for any fieldwork. When faced with this dilemma we began to be interested in the establishment of the school. As policy scholars we were fascinated with how a small school, using an existing policy frame, could elicit such impassioned responses from supporters and opponents. While there had already been research on the controversy around the establishment of the school, much of this research focused on the period of the early to mid-2000s and the final decision to establish in May 2008. We decided to focus on 25 to 30 years before establishment of the school, and work our way to its establishment in 2008. We were intrigued by the multiple instances when Black-focused schooling had been a key issue in Toronto, often connected to race politics in the early 1990s and violence against Black men in the late 1980s, early 1990s and 2000s.

There was something puzzling about the establishment of the school, in that, on the one hand, it appeared a clear-cut example of mobilising school choice for anti-racist purposes, as had been the case with charter schools in the United States; but, on the other hand, it appeared connected to how race, violence, counting and policy were intertwined in a multicultural city. While over seven years have passed since the school opened, we think that focusing on education policy in the emergence of this school can contribute important insights, more generally, into how social and urban policy and difference works in contemporary cities.

For instance, five years after opening, it was reported by a partnership project between York University and the TDSB, that the school was playing an important role in Toronto, namely that:

> The prevailing narrative that emerged was one of a school creating a sense of community for Black people in ways that have not been historically present in public schools and resulted in a distinctly different school climate for Black students, teachers, administrators, parents, and community members. (James et al, 2015: 3)

However, the school continued to face challenges that endured from before the school was established, particularly from negative media and public portrayals of the school. For instance, the 'media attention that the school has received since even before it was established to present day has been quite negative biased, limited, disruptive, and damaging' (James et al, 2015: 44). The mediatisation of contemporary policy illustrates the ways in which a journalistic field represents educational ideas, structures and processes (Lingard and Rawolle, 2004). For our purposes, the way in which representation is used by media is central to understanding how contemporary policy is developed, practised and eventually used. Perhaps even more important for our purposes is the way that the very idea of 'policy' is ushered into fields of intelligibility and significations, and eventually constituted within various discourses and practices.

We have attempted to be reflexive about race, and we use the terms 'African-Canadian' and 'Black' in this book. The former fits the Canadian nomenclature of the hyphenated 'visible minority'. We more commonly use 'Black', and note its usage in the Canadian context, as outlined by Dei and Kempf who contend: 'Even those who consider themselves to be African-Canadian are racialized as Black. So we may embrace Black in both the racialized and politicized sense of the term to allude to victimization, oppression, and resistance' (2013: 24). Another reason for using the term 'Black' is this is what was disputed and contested in the establishment of the Africentric Alternative School, around who was covered by the term 'Africentric' and who was not. 'Black' is used in the politics of race in Toronto locally, and is the term that produces a micropolitics around representation and identification.

The reflexivity about race included our racialised positioning during the research as White, middle-class, male researchers. This caveat reflects the numerous conversations we had about the school. We were asked about what two White, male researchers were doing researching race and schooling in Toronto. We had multiple responses to this question. On the one hand, it was a policy study about the creation of a school, and our work is on race and policy. On the other hand, the school was treated as an outlier within school choice in Canada. As scholars who had examined school choice in the United States, Australia, the United Kingdom and Canada, we wanted to explore more about why some policy choices are okay and others are not.

Our approach to policy and policy studies

This book is a companion to a recent book on doing policy studies, in which we detailed struggles with what is, and what we think should constitute, policy and policy analysis (Webb and Gulson, 2015a). That book attempted to conceptualise what we hoped would be future explorations in policy analysis. We were interested in continuing an idea of 'policy theorists' (Simons et al, 2009: 27), who, following Ball (1994): 'provide ... answers to the epistemological challenges of post-structuralism and the current pluralist social world, and who also take up the difficult work of intellectually-based social criticism'. In this current book we are attempting an empirical companion to what we outlined in the earlier work.[2]

Education can be understood as part of public policy that is 'normative, expressing both ends and means designed to steer the actions and behaviour of people' (Rizvi and Lingard, 2010: 4), and as such involves the authoritative allocation of values (Easton, 1953). Educational policy can be broadly defined as text and processes, and as always encountering ongoing institutional inertias, as well as converging processes and practices, including other forms of public policy (Ball, 1994, 2008; Rizvi and Lingard, 2010). Policy, furthermore, frames both a social or educational problem and its solutions or the responses to it. Policy thus generates 'truths' that can come to be embedded in the common sense of processes and practices associated with schooling (Scheurich, 1994; Bacchi, 2000; Miller and Rose, 2008) – a so-called 'common sense' that elides and masks the complexity, contingency and indeterminacies of policy.

We also want to take note of the affective aspects. The particular aspect of relevance pertains to the policy cycle areas of 'agenda setting' and 'implementation'. While the book may be read as an exploration of the 'agenda setting' and 'implementation' stages of the policy cycle, we are more interested in what might surround these ideas (for more detail on where this approach sits in reference to other forms of policy analysis, see Webb and Gulson, 2015b). This means discussing, for example, implementation as an affective as well as technical undertaking, where affect is 'not installed in somebody or something; rather affectivity is the capacity of influencing on and through somebody/something' (Staunæs and Pors, 2015: 102). This is to see the ways that affect is becoming a key way of both examining governing and a way of governing. As Thrift (2008: 182) notes, 'affect has always been a key element of politics and the subject of numerous powerful political technologies which have knotted thinking, technique and affect together in various potent combinations'.

Our aim in the book is to explore the creation of the Africentric Alternative School from a policy standpoint, but not to make clear distinctions between policy problems and solutions. Rather, we want to examine policy as a problematisation (Bacchi, 2012; Webb, 2014). While Foucault saw problematisation as both a historical governmental practice and a research sensibility,[3] in this book we are focused on the latter. A problematisation is a form of analysis that identifies 'how and why certain things (behaviour, phenomena, processes) became a problem' (Ball, 2013: 28). While this approach to policy analysis is related to the broad field of critical policy analysis in education, we note that there is a tendency in the latter to discursively identify, and assume, hidden contradiction(s) within policy texts, such as competing interests and associated ideologies, that need to be revealed in order for the truth to be known about a policy intent.

Conversely, a policy problematisation politicises the idea of hidden 'truths', including ideas of interests and ideology, by identifying problematic conditions that produce conflicts (Rabinow and Rose, 2003), and identifying education policy practice as manifested in performances and enactments (Ball et al, 2012; Heimans, 2012). Moreover, a problematisation examines the sites of problematic conditions and politicises the conflicts that arise from problematic conditions (rather than, say, attempting to resolve conflicts). Our goal in conducting a policy problematisation, therefore, is to indicate other possible forms of political action that interrupt the conditions that give rise to both 'problems' and the resultant 'solutions' contained in many forms of critical policy analyses (see Simons et al, 2009 for overview).

On data

This book is based on a three-year (2010–13) qualitative project, noted above, on education policy, curriculum, identity and globalisation, and the Africentric Alternative School in Toronto.[4] In some of the chapters 'data' is included as text from interview transcripts and from a variety of other materials. As such, we follow broad ethnographic conventions. However, our approach alters traditional conventions in the ways St Pierre and Jackson (2014: 716) note:

> conventional humanist qualitative research, words in interview transcripts and in field notes are considered primary data, collected as they are in 'face to face' encounters in the *presence* of participants in their natural settings. Again, words spoken by participants are privileged regardless of their adequacy to respond to the study's substantive and theoretical demands.

As St Pierre and Jackson (2014: 716) contend, this view privileges these words over those that might equally be adequate 'to respond to the study's substantive and theoretical demands'. While we accept this critique, we had a slightly different view of this as we undertook the research. We were interested in interviews as a way of engaging with the ideas and concepts that we were forming over the course of the non-interview part of the research.

In 2012, we supplemented the archival work of the project with eight semi-structured interviews with stakeholders including community representatives and TDSB trustees. The latter are elected officials of the school board with a mix of those who voted for and against the school proposal. For reasons of anonymity, in this book we do not indicate how trustees voted and we name all as 'trustees', even if they are ex-members (noting, of course, that in such a study anyone familiar with the trustees as public figures is likely to be able to attribute a position to a trustee). If participants identified with a particular ethnicity, racialised position or culture we have noted this in the excerpts (for example, Black Canadian, Jewish) if we think it matters to the substance of what we are including.

Formal interviews averaged 1.5 hours, with some lasting 2 plus hours and one that lasted 12 minutes. All the interviews were audio taped and transcribed. Some data were organised thematically (for instance, in Chapter Four), but rarely did these assembled ideas serve as codes or analytic constructs for additional analysis. The idea that 'meaning' was buried or lodged within data was not the methodological orientation of this research – given that so much 'meaning' was explicit from the materials that we assembled. Rather, the interviews became both a place to assemble other data with, and ways to problematise, some of our working ideas – even ideas spoken 'within' the transcript.

The interviews attempted and at times succeeded in developing rich and challenging conversations about the development of the Africentric Alternative School. Interestingly, participants developed an enthusiasm during the interviews when we involved them in analysing (see Kvale, 2006), not merely reporting, events and issues surrounding the establishment of the school. At times, the participants reflected that they were discussing these issues to help themselves understand policy and power issues in their work. In fact, several participants responded at some point during the interview that the discussion had been cathartic, needed, and important in attempting to discuss race and multiculturalism in Toronto schooling.

Contested terrain of Black-focused schooling: race and multiculturalism

Race and multiculturalism are significant parts of the story of the Africentric Alternative School. Here we want to provide a brief preface to concepts and issues that we will explore in more detail throughout the book.

We start with reference to the way that a proposed focus on Africentric schooling and curricula were rejected as being a form of exclusive rather than inclusive education. This rejection was premised on an accusation that Afrocentric schooling uses a flawed notion of a unitary Black identity (Lund, 1998). The primary opposition to the establishment of Afrocentric schools similarly mobilised notions of separation, framing the Africentric Alternative School as a move to re-segregate the public school system. The spectre of segregation had been raised repeatedly and historically in the context of Black-focused schools (James, 2011), for example, when the Toronto school board was deliberating whether to approve the opening of the Africentric Alternative School.

> Before the trustees' vote in January 2008, the media, which has played a significant part in perpetuating the segregation myth, also weighed in as all three major Toronto dailies condemned the proposal. The *Toronto Star* argued the 'idea smacks of segregation, which is contrary to the values of the school system and Canadian society as a whole,' while the Globe and Mail ran a column that called black-focused schools 'as insulting as they are ridiculous.' Even more vehement in its criticism, the *National Post* said the 'concept of special schools for black students is one of those terrible ideas that refuses to die'. (Wallace, 2009)

For some opponents, both Black and non-Black, enunciations of segregation were redolent of historical and geographical separation. Black schooling, thus, represented a reprise of formal, racialised schooling in North America, the histories and geographies of slavery in Canada and the USA, and the doctrine of 'separate but equal' in the USA. The spectre of separation, when enunciated as part of opposition to the school, occluded the ways in which low student achievement or historical exclusion for Black students had been endemic within public schooling; that is, raising segregation was a way for whiteness to be reinscribed as normative within public schools (James, 2011).

Conversely, school choice policy that enabled the establishment of Black-focused schooling produced different enunciations of place and belonging, and different mobilisations of segregation. For instance, the enunciation of segregation had been co-opted by advocates of Black-focused schools. Dei (1995) took the racialised history of segregation and reconfigured it, asserting there was a difference between segregation by force and segregation by choice. Dei contended that: 'For those that argue that having … Black-focused schools is going back to the days of segregation, it should be noted that there is a qualitative difference between "forced segregation" and "segregation by choice"' (Dei, 1995: 186).

Black-focused schools in Toronto, therefore, were part of both school choice decisions, and what forms of separation become marked as 'other'. In a highly charged educational political environment in Toronto, the proposed Africentric school was assembled as separate in ways that other forms of 'alternative' schools were not – including girls' schools, lesbian, gay, bisexual, transgender schools and so forth (James, 2011). When opposition to Black-focused schooling raised issues of segregation and separation it denoted the continued saliency of race and racism in Canada, and the connection to the complex and contested terrain of multiculturalism and anti-racism.

The reactions to the school 'forced [us] to think about why racism persists and quickly resurfaces even when thought to be thoroughly dismantled, about the play between endurance and change' (Amin, 2010: 2). In part, the temporalities of race were connected to the Africentric Alternative School as representing an important event of racial recognition in the multicultural registers of Canada, perhaps even a moment of 'strategic essentialism' (Danius et al 1993). We were intrigued by the school, which seemed to be about both anti-racism and about multiculturalism in a city like Toronto 'sometimes hailed as the most diverse city in the world' (Goonewardena and Kipfer, 2005: 670). The persistence of race seemed connected to the multiple ways in which multiculturalism plays out in Canada (more on this in Chapter Five).

Briefly, first, multiculturalism is a way for governments to manage and control difference (Mitchell, 2003). Second, Canadian multiculturalism is premised on the notion of 'colour-blindness', that actively works to deny the status of race and racism in the project of the nation (Mackey, 1999). In the framework of colour-blind multiculturalism (Mackey, 1999; James, 2011), Black-focused schools can be seen as 'un-Canadian'. That is, Black-focused schools can be opposed for they contravene the assertion that race is absent in Canada. The assertion that race is absent denies a history of Black slaves in Canada and the demolishing in the 1960s of identifiably Black urban areas such as Africville in Nova Scotia (Nelson, 2008). The opposition to the Africentric Alternative School converts the assertion of political power and the need to address systemic historical disadvantage into a threat to national identity.

Market forms of education, such as school choice, are connected to a third way to understand Canadian multiculturalism as neoliberal multiculturalism, where stated 'new cultural rights and neoliberal political economic reforms' are combined (Hale, 2005: 28). This occurs when identities are articulated and recognised in education markets as a corrective to 'colour-blind' multiculturalism, when markets become a form of anti-racism.

These three permutations of 'multiculturalism' all attempt to resuscitate the liberal state. And yet, as Grosz notes, perhaps such permutations are not enough:

> Rethinking multiculturalism and antiracism, conceptualizing them in terms that facilitate social, political and economic change, entails the creation of more thoroughly radical concepts, concepts with a less invested, and with perhaps a wider, range than that afforded by the regime of recognition. (Grosz, 2002: 463)

We suggest here that racial biopolitics is one such concept that troubles or problematises 'the regime of recognition' that structures any ideas of multiculturalism. What we are interested in, and why we have foregrounded the idea of racial biopolitics in the title of this book, is that we are convinced that understanding the emergence of the Africentric Alternative School can be understood through racial biopolitics in ways that are different from a focus on anti-racism and multiculturalism. As Amin proposes:

> it is the interplay between vernacular habits with long historical roots of reading racial and social worth from surface bodily differences and racial biopolitics that makes the critical difference to the real experience of race, arbitrating the choice between accommodation and discipline of the racialized other. (Amin, 2010: 3–4)

For racial biopolitics gets us to a place where we can talk about why violence still matters, and why the contemporary (as at time of writing) Black Lives Matter movement resonates with what Black community members were arguing for in Toronto in the 1980s, 1990s and 2000s. It gets us towards why phenotypes still seem to be racialised as opposed to merely visual markers of difference. We explore these ideas in more detail throughout the book.

Book organisation: on starting in the middle

If you are looking for a neat explanation for the establishment of the Africentric Alternative School there is not one to be found here. In this book we are attempting what Brinkmann (2014) characterises as abductive reasoning:

> [u]nlike induction and deduction – both of which address the relationship between data and theory – abduction is a form of reasoning that is concerned with the relationship between a situation and inquiry. It is neither data-driven nor theory driven, but breakdown driven (Alvesson and Kärreman, 2011). It occurs in situations of breakdown, surprise, bewilderment, or wonder. (2014: 722)

We think that what we are attempting to do is to undertake analysis that occurs '"through the middle" (Deleuze and Guattari, 1987 [1980]: 293), without a beginning or end, without origin or destination. In this way, analysis occurs *everywhere and all the time*' (St Pierre and Jackson, 2014: 717). As will become clear, we deal with multiple examples that seem singular, but explore them not as a causal chain, rather to see if a particular form of generalisability will emerge. Like Berlant (2011: 12) we are interested in the idea of generalisability as 'how the singular becomes delaminated from its location in someone's story or some locale's irreducibly local history and circulated as evidence of something shared'. As such, in the case of the Africentric Alternative School, we are hopeful that we may be able to map 'the becoming general of singular things' (Berlant, 2011: 12).

We use four major ideas, or preconditions, to relay our account of the school, in addition to the idea of an event. These ideas are: biopolitics, neoliberalism, the politics of recognition, and the city and its relationships to race and multiculturalism. Each idea is discussed in a separate chapter and in relation to a significant policy event that precipitated the becoming of the Africentric Alternative School. Our choice of ideas and events is not designed to be exhaustive. Rather, our selections are motivated by four ideas that we believe radically problematise normative conceptions of education policy, race and liberal multiculturalism. Further, our use of these ideas problematise what has been absent from earlier accounts of the school's becoming.

The absences, we contend, are primarily produced by an adherence to particular Enlightenment ideals that generate preferred accounts of both education policy and anti-racist projects. These preferred accounts simultaneously obfuscate alternative renderings of events, and specifically do not account for how several of our selected ideas operate in order to facilitate the illusion of Enlightenment ideals. In addition, our selections are designed to be instructive in relation to education policy generally, and in relation to policy events specifically. Finally, the separation of events and ideas into chapters is artificial and dictated by the format of a book for accessibility, convenience and intelligibility.

Chapter One provides an overview of the types of accounts of the Africentric school. It also serves as a methodological chapter about the structure of the book as a split text, and provides an initial insight into the ways our four-year research about the Africentric Alternative School revealed at least 3,000 policy events that were instrumental in the school's becoming. The chapter examines, and provides different conceptualisations on, how one defines 'events' and 'eventalisation' as being critical to how one arrives at such a number. The chapter highlights how it is safe to say that we identified and analysed far more events than could possibly be recast into a book; and, moreover, the important events that followed the arrival of the school were not documented.

Chapter Two connects race-based statistics to race-based violence, ideas of counting and racial biopolitics. The focus is on two events. The first is a 2008 a report into school safety, the *Falconer report* (SCSAP, 2008), which advocated for the use of 'race-based statistics' in the TDSB and reignited the overall move towards Black-focused schooling. We connect this report, and its plea to use race-based statistics in discipline-related incidents in schooling, to racial profiling and policing in Toronto in the early 2000s. The chapter concludes with the TDSB decision in 2004–5, to collect limited types of race-based statistics, not including suspensions and expulsions, as a second policy event that preceded the *Falconer report*.

Chapter Three uses the idea of educational neoliberalism in relation to the alternative school policies of the TDSB. We note how ideas of 'choice' conjoined previously opposed political ideologies and illustrate how ideas of choice have radically altered notions of justice in education policy, including a refashioning of policy subjects and policy objects. We identify how education policy overlaps neoliberalism with new forms of privatised racisms, and forms of entrepreneurialism and commodification.

Chapter Four discusses the idea of a racialised and multicultural city in relation to a the decision about where to locate the Africentric Alternative School. We show how the city itself is a powerful force in shaping educational policy. The city of Toronto was powerfully shaped by various racial, spatial and economic factors that ostensibly functioned as forceful preconditions for the becoming of the school. This chapter examines the event of finding a location for the school, and the connections between the ways in which the city was (and is) racialised and undergoing urban change around gentrification and 'rebranding' of neighbourhoods. We identify the connections between education policy, cities, race and ethnicity, and the new forms of suburbia in multicultural cities.

Chapter Five discusses the politics of recognition in relation to broader anti-racist practices, and specifically discusses how these ideas were brought to bear upon the TDSB after the shooting and death of a grade nine student, Jordan Manners. We show how the shooting deaths of several Black men in Toronto were absorbed into policy regimes that affected the becoming of the school. Moreover, we show how impermanent ideas of recognition, representation and difference strongly steered policy making that ultimately produced the school.

Our conclusion notes the benefits and costs of our 'more ontological' approach to understanding the becoming of the school. Specifically, we address how our particular analysis of education policy can be used to map constellations of power and force that have a large degree of influence over policy subjects and policy actors. We examine school choice as part of living in desperate times and the fraught politics of market approaches to equity. Our approach to policy analysis, then, is not designed to trace particular decisions nor to illustrate contradictions. Rather, our ontological approach is an attempt to ferret out some of the important preconditions that shape our endless attempts at racial justice. As such, we conclude the book by asking whether the Africentric Alternative School is the mark of a racial biopolitics or a post-racial future for the multicultural cities.

How to...

This book is comprised of an introduction and six chapters. Five of these chapters contain a 'subtext', with the final chapter, our conclusion, not participating in this mechanic. The subtexts were written to operate as 'a series of separate texts that resonate, run along, interfere with, alienate from, and give an extra dimension to the main text' (Mol, 2002: 3). Our subtexts, then, are designed to deliberately introduce problematisations of specific concepts that are introduced in the 'first' part of each chapter. Our subtexts are also designed to remind readers about how we relate to academic literature, and the dangers lurking within ideas of representation, especially as practised in language and within the practices of signification and raciology in particular.

Our subtexts, then, are designed to introduce a non/representational element to our study. Here, our idea of non/representation is oriented along what Anderson and Harrison (2010) suggested as attempts to capture or affirm the multiplicities produced within representations. Our use of non/representation is not a simple rejection of representation, a reading of 'non' as 'anti' representation. In other words, our use of subtexts is a way to affirm and enact the performative nature of representation that is often neglected, and particularly neglected, in academic writing. Like Mol (2002), our subtexts were written to enact a jarring experience: to set up a direct opposition to the cosy confines of reading narrative exposition so often practised in educational research.

Each subtext is introduced within the body of the main text with the use of the ⋆ symbol. In addition, each subtext has been given a title to introduce it; these titles are not included in the Table of Contents as each subtext is a part of the chapter that contains it. Unlike Mol (2002) and Petersen (2015), our subtexts are not placed in the space usually reserved for footnotes. Ours are placed as continuous to the chapters to which they adhere, but distinguished by a different font from the text that precedes it.

Notes

1. We use the term 'Africentric' in reference to the Alternative School, and Afrocentric in reference to either Afrocentric schooling more broadly, or Afrocentric as a body of thought.
2. Our thanks to our friend and colleague Eva Bendix Petersen for challenging us to undertake this approach.
3. With thanks to an anonymous reviewer for this point.
4. This research was supported by the Social Sciences and Humanities Research Council of Canada.

ONE

Policy events

This book is another account of how the Africentric Alternative School came to be, and an account of how policy, race and multicultural cities are enmeshed. There are several published public and academic accounts of how the school came to be. In fact, the becoming of the Africentric Alternative School was one of the most mediatised events in Canadian history. Mainstream media interviewed hundreds of people about the possibility of establishing the school. Online and print media reported on several community and school district meetings on whether or not the school should become. Numerous debates were televised about Black-focused schooling in general, and the emergence of the school in particular. International media produced a constant stream of moralising editorials about the possibility of the school. Comments in the blogosphere, supporting and opposing the school, were virtually impossible to count due to the sheer volume of thoughts about something not quite arrived.

A few published accounts of the school's becoming exist in academia – a book and journal article here, a graduate thesis there. At least two documentary movies were made on how the school came to be. Additionally, the Toronto District School Board (TDSB) possessed reams of published material – organised and sanitised as the official record and available online as minutes – on how the school became. Accounts of the school's creation were informally discussed around dinner tables, demanded through megaphones on city streets, whispered in the hallways of the school district. These unpublished accounts, these anecdotes that reinforced that something was happening, would sometimes find their way into published accounts; but, more often than not, these unpublished accounts would evaporate like the morning mist above one of the great lakes adjoining the fourth largest school district in North America. Among all these accounts, this book is one more about how the school came to be, but it is a book that is interested in policy, racial biopolitics and the city specifically. It is this that sets it apart from other accounts.

There are several reasons for the numerous public accounts of the school's becoming. Some reasons are obvious; for instance, the fact that Toronto is a heavily mediatised city. The media machine needs to produce stories, and the possibility of an Africentric Alternative

School was an event* 'controversial' enough to attract customers. Other obvious reasons include the fact that different people had different perspectives and different investments in relation to the process of becoming a school. A teacher, parent, reporter, citizen, homeowner, trustee, student and community activist were distributed differentially within, and across, the many time-spaces of the school's becoming. And, to make things a bit more complicated, people inhabited multiple (identity) categories by virtue of living as a parent *and* teacher, or homeowner *and* community activist. Different and multiple representational and material locations produced different and multiple accounts.

Other reasons for the varied accounts of the school's becoming rest upon the murky idea of what it means for a school to become, and when and where that happens. Does acquiring physical space constitute a school? Does a 'mission statement' or an 'education philosophy' constitute a school? Does a school become when it is first discussed at a board meeting? Or does a school become when the idea is discussed in a cafe prior to a board meeting? Or does a school become when it is imagined in policy documents *twenty-five years* before a board decision?

Numerous preconditions – political and social movements, policy activists, and so forth – involved with establishing the school meant a large number of accounts were produced. Preconditions were set well in advance of the becoming of the Africentric Alternative School, and not necessarily for the purposes of establishing the school. As such, people worked in and around these preconditions, either in attempts to establish the school or to halt its becoming. Moreover, these preconditions powerfully shaped people's accounts of the school. As we will show, there was not a single process to the becoming of the Africentric Alternative School. In fact, there were many processes and preconditions that shaped the event; processes and preconditions that powerfully shaped how people accounted for the school.

Less obvious reasons for the numerous accounts of the school's becoming rest with different histories people have in relation to what the school might become. That is a tricky sentence, one that links multiple and different histories with multiple and different futures. For example, the Africentric Alternative School was imbued with the hopes of people who had pasts with schooling – and the city of Toronto – that were unequal, repressive, and that required advocacy for change. Here, accounts of the Africentric Alternative School were aspirational, even inspirational. Of course, there were accounts of the Africentric Alternative School that were infused with disdain and fear, in attempts to produce the school's non-becoming, or hopeful demise. A few accounts were perhaps even ambivalent, but told with the assumption that a school becoming would be yet another complicated event in a city that never stopped moving.

Accounting for race and racism

The major impetus for the numerous accounts of the school's becoming were related to ideas of race, anti-Black racism and multiculturalism. As noted in the Introduction, the Africentric Alternative School could be considered a Canadian precursor to the contemporary North American politics of recognition, Black Lives Matter. A politics of recognition attempts to provide dignity to, and is claimed by, groups who have been historically marginalised or historically unrecognised. Recognition acknowledges the presence and worth of groups who have been historically marginalised by those in power. Some accounts of the Africentric school's becoming are situated within these recognitive politics.

Canadian politics of recognition, however, faces different challenges than the same politics practised south of its border. The largest challenge comes from the insistence on multicultural policies that deny conceptions of race, and hence obfuscate acts of racism. Canada's multicultural policies are infused with a 'post-race' ideology that treats race as a biologically random variation or a biological antecedent, and markedly contrasts with the centrality of race to public life in the United States. In Canada, therefore, random variations in which racism is a causal factor in disadvantage have no place in social policy, particularly education policy, and especially not with reference to the possibilities of establishing a new school. Ironically, several accounts of the school described its becoming *as an act of racism itself* due to using the annulled concept of race within the 'post-race' registers of Canada's multicultural policies. For instance, some accounts treated the school as a painful homage to educational segregation – a curious form of neo-segregation through self-exile.

Canada's romance with 'post-race' multiculturalism alters the recognitive messages of Black Lives Matter into a naïve humanist message of 'All Lives Matter'. This code switch is the latest symptom of a social disease in Canada that disciplines racial politics, while conveniently maintaining the power arrangements of the great White north. For instance, Canada's current (and historical) use of a pointedly anti-Black term (the 'n-word') to name several geographical places (these places are currently being renamed) reveals a haunting and ignorant racist past (Anonymous, 2015). The code switch tries to align its 'post-racial' multicultural policies with excuses that rewrite the meaning of the term as an 'inconsequential name' used to identify 'meaningless places'. Aside from the denigrations smuggled within geography, Canadian Jim Crow laws, the slave trade in Quebec, and lynchings of Black people in Ontario all attest to what contemporary Canadian accounts try to deny and/or deflect to south of the border.

In essence, this code switch legitimises and perpetuates anti-Black racist practices. 'All Lives Matter', a White multiculturalism, misunderstands anti-Black racism (and specifically misunderstands and ignores institutional forms of racism). The code switch subverts important messages about recognising specific lives that have not mattered in Canada, and that continue to struggle for recognition and dignity today. The becoming of the Africentric Alternative School can be considered not just as the creation of a safe physical and representational place within the contradictory spaces of Canada's anti-Black racism and education, but part of the ongoing effort to introduce a racial politics of recognition and dignity in Canada. Black Lives Matter in Canada too.

Lost in translation: recognition and representation

However, other accounts of the Africentric Alternative School considered the school to be a failed attempt in a sorrowful lineage of recognitive justice. Some accounts of the event noticed how vague ideas of 'identity' and 'representation' were marshalled to argue for the school. These accounts raised questions about the very ideas of 'identities', including school and racial identities. Furthermore, these accounts questioned who determined who belonged – and who didn't – to these respective identifications. Some of these accounts argued that phenotypes and identities were contingent, and inextricably interconnected, markers of life, recognised through performative acts that transmitted coded messages to others for acceptance and belonging.

These accounts reduced whatever status the school had as symbol of racial justice, and transformed the school into an object aligned with the historical discourses of 'entitlements' and 'identity politics'. What does it mean to be recognised? Are declarations of identity equivalent to recognition? Is some kind of reciprocity assumed (that is, desired) within recognition attempts?

More importantly, what forms of power regulate and distribute recognitive attempts; and to what extent do these forms of power differentiate life prospects? A few accounts of the school's becoming noted that, notwithstanding problems of identity and identification, a politics of recognition remains ultimately servile to the very groups solicited for recognition. A politics of recognition remains governed by the dominant (that is, by White supremacy).

There are, of course, other forms of politics, not just humanist forms, that utilise recognition, identification and representation as key tropes. One alternative politics would be one that seeks alterations to the very structures that recognise and produce people (and representations thereof). Within such a politics, realigning different forces and concomitant systems of power is central to rearranging the spaces, such as governmental and educational spaces, in order to produce a more just world. If schools themselves are sites that practice and generate various forms of racism in Canada, such as institutional racisms, then might an alternative politics not be about the *improvement* of schools (that is, school reform) or *which kinds* of schools (that is, school choice); rather the question might be *whether or not schools should exist at all?* Would claiming a dedicated space of racial recognition and racial integrity counteract the racist practices of the very institution it would soon become? Or, would new raciologies emerge from this indeterminate and paradoxical space?

The city as a racialised marketplace

While Canada's multicultural policies actively seek to eliminate registers of racial recognition, the becoming of the Africentric Alternative School was recognised as a legitimate educational site through educational economics, and school-choice policies. Educational markets ostensibly provide people with a sense of agency, perhaps even a powerful sense of control through entrepreneurial activities. The school might provide a moment of revolutionary impact and an interruption into a history of school choice that has primarily benefited the White, middle classes, but likely would be recaptured into the Enlightenment's machines of racism, colonisation and global capital. The contradictions of the Enlightenment project, where equality is presumed (and required) but belied through various practices of slavery and segregation, gendered and sexual limitations, and explicitly racist formulations (for example, phrenology) will, likely, not cease through a singular act of identifying or 'reclaiming' one of these contradictions. At least not through using the Enlightenment's sorting machine, the school.

The becoming of the Africentric Alternative School rests upon questions about what constitutes a school, and, more importantly, what constitutes a school within educational markets that, now, enunciate different raciologies. Can school-choice policies and educational entrepreneurs end racism in Canada, as was presumed to be the case in the United States through charter schools? Was educational economics the only politics available to fight anti-Black racism? Would the racial category of 'Black' be commodified in these emerging markets?

The city is important to the recognitive becoming of the Africentric Alternative School. Many accounts of the school's becoming hinted at Toronto's racialised geography. Ethnic terms designate micro-geographies within the city; for instance, 'Chinatown', 'Greektown', 'Little Manilla' and 'Little Italy' are ways Toronto is arranged. The city's history is also mapped by terms that are less racial in denotation, for instance, 'Southside', 'Eastside', and 'The Ward' (Jewish); but nevertheless, these terms connote important racialised and ethnic areas (see Chapter Four).

Many cities around the world are mapped with similar racial and ethnic terms. In this sense, the city performs a kind recognitive politics – at least in name. But to what extent do racialised locales within cities 'recognise' groups or, instead, stigmatise racial 'ghettos' using a feigned sense of recognition like a patronising 'pat on the head'? A few accounts described the Africentric school as a racial sanctuary within the city, and as a place to deliberately separate from the dominant and oppressive forms of White power that govern Toronto.

Toronto's choice schools are situated within detailed histories of race and various racisms. A few accounts of the school hinted at the city's histories with race and anti-Black racism. Other accounts mentioned the city in relation to the uneven incomes that maintained Toronto's racial and economic striations, and the racialised imaginaries of different parts of the city. For instance, where the school would be located produced heated accounts of the school's becoming. Of course, school-choice policies operated within the racialised and emerging geographies of the city. Policies do not operate in a vacuum but in concert, within the city's histories. Hence, the city – with all of its racial history and racialised geographies (and all of its racial futures) – was the 'marketplace' for the becoming of the Africentric Alternative School.

Race and anti-Black racism would be recognised through the various registers supporting Toronto's educational markets, and recognised through registers of the city's racial histories and racial geographies. What does it mean to become a policy entrepreneur within the racialised markets of school choice? Do policy entrepreneurs replace the void of educational equality forsaken by governments? Or do policy entrepreneurs unwittingly perpetuate capitalist raciologies and racisms? Both? Is it the case that education policy simultaneously produces equality *and* racism?

The lives and deaths of education policy

Schools, race, policies and the city functioned as important preconditions to the event of the Africentric Alternative School. In other words, the becoming of the school was affected through this set of preconditions, and in combination with a few others. At different times, these preconditions mediated *how* people lived and, more importantly, *which* people lived. In other words, the preconditions ostensibly functioned to administer, influence and control the lives of different populations. Preconditions, then, grafted the living of a life with different political techniques used to administer different populations. Education policy is a good example of this. The idea of race is another example of how populations are controlled. A few accounts of the Africentric Alternative School mentioned the essential relationships between political life (that is, schools, race, policies and cities) and living a life.

But are these relationships essential? What alternative preconditions might be fashioned for living a life? What political forms are necessary to develop those alternatives? Accounts that acknowledged various preconditions of the school's becoming hinted at the different kinds of political techniques used to govern different populations (for example, deprivation, established standards, defined norms, therapeutics, optimisation and so on). Nevertheless, most accounts of the school hinted that, without the preconditions of schools, race, policies and the city, life '*as we know it*' would quickly cease. As we will show, some accounts noted that the becoming of the Africentric Alternative School was a matter of living and dying for Black students in Toronto within the current arrangements of contemporary life. The maintenance of these current preconditions obfuscated the search for alternative preconditions *to live life differently*. As such, the politics of searching for alternative preconditions violently clashed with the political techniques used to administer contemporary life and death.

Anti-racism attempts to ameliorate the Enlightenment project by applying universalist and idealist assumptions about humans (that is, equal) and society (that is, progress) in recognitive and representative ways. However, these assumptions and practices actively suppress alternative anti-racist activities designed to understand how bodies are materially differentiated into hierarchies in the first place. Our account of the Africentric Alternative School emphasises the links between race, schooling and capitalist governance in order to highlight the contradictions of the Enlightenment project through the particular practices of the school: as we have noted, the school is the central machine in the Enlightenment's contradictory project. In other words, our account maps how racial phenotypes are posited, organised, practised and desired within conflicting forms of state governance and educational markets.

Our account illustrates how racial phenotypes are splayed across a canvas of universalist and idealist logics of the Enlightenment project that constitute our current understandings of human difference and human representation. More importantly, our account attends to the ways these contemporary racial ontologies, and the continued significance of racialised bodies and objects, function within educational contexts of neoliberalism and school choice, the *conditio sine qua non* of political modernity.

Our goal is to illustrate how race and racism are multitudinous processes that – once factors of neoliberalism, biopolitics and non/representation are accounted for – produce paradoxical terrains of anti-racist approaches in education.

This book might not be educational research

Amid the cacophony of noise before and after the establishment of the school, why would we add additional accounts to how the Africentric Alternative School came to be? In order to answer that question, it is important to explain why we chose to describe the above as *accounts*, rather than say 'stories', 'narratives', 'voice(s)', 'evidence', 'data' or 'research' – terms that are popular in our field of work. An account, after all, is a report of an event. The Africentric Alternative School did not contain a neat narrative 'beginning' or 'conclusion'. As we will show, the Africentric Alternative School does not fit a convenient timeline. In fact, the event of the Africentric Alternative School is impossible to fit in any chronology.

A narrative, for the most part, concocts a timeline as an artifice to retell an event. This is done for reasons related to expediency, as the retelling of an event may never end (and by extension, never begin). For instance, stories and narratives typically contain a linear sense of time that involves an exposition, problem or conflict, a denouement and/or a resolution. For example, a few narrative accounts placed the school's becoming within social disruption, known as the Yonge Street Riot and a subsequent White Paper entitled *Towards a new beginning* (Ontario Government/African Canadian Community Working Group, 1992). Other narratives focused on particular actors – educational entrepreneurs – and how they used the district's alternative school policies circa 2003 to establish the school. Or we could posit that the school's becoming was intertwined within the colonial economies that relied upon the Atlantic slave trade. The event of the school's becoming will, inevitably, never end. That is, even when the school is closed, it will remain as a memory, as a statement against, and disruption of, anti-Black racism, and as a policy artefact. Narrative conceptions of the school's becoming also produced accounts that used the school as a kind of conclusion to the Conservative ideology of the Mike Harris government (1995–2002); as a denouement to the many different discriminatory practices found within the separate school boards prior to the amalgamation into the TDSB; and, as an end to the anti-Black racism perpetuated through Canada's 'post-racial' multicultural policies of non-recognition.

In this sense, narratives are superb in isolating specific factors. To do so, narratives enclose events with arbitrary claims of time, and arbitrary designations of place. Arbitrary does not mean false; rather, the use of the term *arbitrary* signals creative licence with important ideas of time and space. For instance, while the becoming of the school occurred in Toronto in a particular board meeting, it is also occurred in cafes, private homes, community centres, school district offices, and was televised to the world. Or the becoming of the Africentric Alternative School occurred in the Atlantic Ocean. As an event, the Africentric Alternative School occurred in many different locales, in differing times. In moments of 'creative licence', narratives delimit events to fit temporal and spatial structures for retellings.

Nesbitt (2013: 2) remarked:

> the critique of racism, colonization, or global capital, must take into account the *a priori*, transcendental determinants that allow for the taking place of such processes of subjection and exploitation, as well as the flight from those situations by novel subjects of emancipation (collective or individual), the becoming-minoritarian and becoming-other, the subtractive politics of constituting other worlds.

Our account tries to capture some of the determinants of educational policy's temporal and spatial events that narratives and many forms of educational research either avoid, ignore, substantially minimise or simply accept. Our account identifies the 'transcendental determinants' of biopolitics, neoliberalism, recognition and representation, and the multicultural city that strongly influenced the becoming of the school. Our account, then, derives from an ontological inquiry into policy rather than primarily an epistemological one.

Accounts are not always told in the past tense, but often, especially in policy studies, relayed *during* the event. In fact, events may last hundreds of years and accounts are retellings often trapped within temporal sequences that do not fit traditional ideas of time contained within the obligatory narrative readings of the 'past, present and future'. Accounts of events are actually enactments during events. It is a curious feature of accounts that they try to stand apart from the very events which enact the account. In this sense, accounts of the school's becoming can be simultaneously accounts of the Harris government, the amalgamation of six school districts, *and* of colonial economics. Events contain multiple times, where important past and future meanings are entangled within the unfolding of events themselves.

Hence, different and competing conceptions of time and space are used politically, and as part of social movements in cities. Politics, in this sense, is the result of struggle over the depiction of events. The political challenge, therefore, is to discern between accounts that are inextricably intertwined with the perceptions and memories of the very event in question. Our interest has been *why* people accounted for the school and *in what ways*. In other words: in what ways did both educational research and different narrative accounts construct different temporal and spatial arrangements of the school's becoming? Why? For what purposes? Several accounts of the school, both for and against, simply added more sanctimony to an already overflowing moral river about schooling. How might our account look to the ways in which reconstructing time and space can alter powers and forces in order to live differently?

In similar fashion, educational research contains artifices to assist itself. The major artifice in educational research is 'knowledge' and how it is conceptualised within formations of an additional artifice: 'science'. For instance, research often tries to 'stand outside' an object, but the 'objectivity' of social phenomena is an idea that only denigrates the tricky and important role of perception, memory, the emotional lives of people, and the politics and problems of events themselves. Most research attempts to 'disseminate its findings' in ways that try to legitimate different truth claims to be used elsewhere, for example *for* or *on* other people. Here, educational research uses the artifices of 'knowledge' and 'science' to make claims about supposed truths.

Hence, another reason we chose the term 'accounts' is due to the scepticism that the term denotes. On one hand, this scepticism alters a traditional genealogical understanding of events that strives for a specific origin, a single cause or single conclusion. Accounts, on the other hand, provide for the possibility of multiple truths and a plurality of understandings within events. In this sense, accounts specifically capture some of the (immense) variability within the retelling of events.

Summary

We use accounts in this book to provide opportunities to note the inconsistencies between and across event records. However, inconsistencies are not necessarily basis for falsification. Rather, inconsistencies provide opportunities for additional accounts, additional 'truths' and additional understandings. Unfortunately, the term 'account' is usually deployed to discredit or disprove rival retellings. We instead use the term in ways that reflect the multiplicities contained within an event. It is the multiplicity of accounts, and the multiplicities of 'truths', that we wish to capture, and that we aim to explore through each of the chapters that follow.

Policy in/compossibles

*Why would we describe the becoming of the Afrocentric Alternative School as an event? What is an event? The preferred term of 'case study' would likely be more applicable qua educational research. We might drill further and describe our account as a *particularistic* case study, or as a *qualitative* or *descriptive* case study. We might have even described our account as a *heuristic* case study in order to assist others establish a similar school. These kinds of scientific discourses certainly sound appropriate and authoritative for our purposes. Hence, why discuss the becoming of the Africentric Alternative School as an event?

At this point we have used the term 'event' in a manner consistent with its general use: *something that happens, usually of some importance.* Given the attention paid to the school's becoming, this definition might be sufficient in and of itself. However, the term has a more nuanced account within some academic literatures. Nuances that better assist us explain our account of the school's becoming, and nuances that better assist us explain our roles and purposes for conducting the study.

However, how should we discuss and use the literature that supports and guides our account? Should we ignore questions about theory, methodology and perspective? If we did, this text would likely not be published as an academic work. Failure to account for questions of theory, methodology and perspective would also neglect the rich experiences of many people and other objects involved with the school's becoming.

Annemarie Mol (2002) discussed her dissatisfaction with the ways academic literature is used. Mol explained that citations often (1) lack specifics, or generalise; (2) conflate and/or simplify different ideas or traditions of thought; (3) obscure their own use or function (for example, as support or as contrast); (4) alter the meaning of disciplinary knowledge within interdisciplinary registers (and vice versa); (5) limit access to libraries, different languages ; and (6) misrepresent authorial commitments.

Is it possible to use the academic literature in ways that do not alienate or confuse readers, and that might actually inform readers? More importantly, is it possible to use the academic literature in ways that do not reproduce the reductive, generalising and misrepresentative functions of academic literature?

Mol used the textual space dedicated for footnotes to discuss the literature she used in her study. More importantly, Mol discussed the literature in ways that did not reproduce the reductive, generalising and misrepresentative aspects of academic literature.

Rather, she produced 'a series of separate texts that resonate, run along, interfere with, alienate from, and give an extra dimension to the main text. In a subtext, so to speak' (2002: 3). Petersen (2015) had a similar aim in the use of a split/ text that aimed to destabilise and question the claims made in the 'above', 'main', or 'only' text. We have borrowed these ideas and developed a subtext that follows a 'first' text.

For instance, take the idea of an event. We use this idea throughout this chapter, and yet, we have not yet provided a definition. Given the genre that we are working with (that is, an academic book), we could devote a few paragraphs, perhaps even an entire chapter, within the body of the text to discuss the idea of an event, its academic lineage, and the affordances and problems it provides. We might call this chapter our 'theoretical framework' and/or 'methodology'.

However, a few paragraphs would be insufficient to discuss the idea. An entire chapter might be sufficient; however, it would interrupt the rhythm of the book. We could write a chapter about the idea of 'event' and instruct readers to skip it if they wanted to. But clearly we must revisit how to relate to the literature; if we write portions of a book to be skipped, what is the point?

Explications of ideas rarely provide readers with insights into the kinds of relationships authors have to ideas, and tend to be dry, analytic and often elide the relationships. At best, readers infer a thin form of identification from the citations authors use in texts (and infer a great deal from these considered 'clues'). At worst, authors remain unaware that citations connote affiliation. Our subtext, conversely, aims to provides a space to reflect on the academic literature we have used. Further, we use a variety of ideas to support our account of the school's becoming, not just the idea of an *event*, but other ideas like *neoliberalism, biopolitics, problematisation* and *non/representation*. We decided it was too unwieldy to write separate chapters on each idea, and not worth our time to ask readers to avoid such chapters if written.

More importantly, our decision to use these ideas is deliberate, and our relationships to these ideas, to theory and theorising, are in tension and problematic. We believe it is too easy to select literature that obfuscates the problematics and contradictions of academic work, and that this is disingenuous with regard to readers who invest their time and energies in writing and reading academic work.

We use Mol's and Petersen's examples for the reasons described above. We do so in order to avoid reducing and generalising ideas and people. Thanks to Mol and Petersen, we are aware of how academic literature often generalises and misrepresents ideas. As such, our use of a supplementary text also provides us with an emblematic and functional space to highlight the embedded notions of representation when working with ideas of race, racism and raciologies. Representation is a key concern in studies of race and an integral aspect in the function of multicultural policies in liberal democracies.

We take the ideas of representation seriously when relaying our account of the school's becoming, and this mechanic provides us with ways to do that. We want to critique ideas of representation because we believe that these ideas no longer function in the ways that they were intended; or, to put it more critically, these ideas are functioning in highly efficient ways that prevent and obfuscate democratic projects.

Event

The disciplines of philosophy and history have long discussed the nature of events, including the meaning of the term and attempts to develop precision around its use. The discussion is predicated on better understanding how intentions are developed, and, it is assumed, used to make changes to the world.

Changes to the world often occur in relation to remedying a problematic situation. As such, elaborate theories of causality have been developed through discussions of events, perhaps most evident in the popular logic that emanates from the phrase 'What triggered the event?' For instance, how would an Africentric Alternative School function as a remedy to anti-Black racism in education? In the hope of it being identified as central to reproduction or change, and hence being replicable, the event has become an important concept in social theory and in policy studies. However, much of this discussion is located in Newtonian and Cartesian conceptions of science used to determine events and their respective causes and effects. Moreover, it privileges the roles of human intention and causality; that is, humans as the centre of change.

Instead, in this book our interest in events is focused upon what enacts humans, and in the many ways humans are enacted through events. As Patton (1997: np) noted, 'the conceptualisation of new events enables us to become conscious of processes and forces at work in the present, those which we might seek to advance as well as those we might oppose'. Specifically, our interest in events is designed to understand how people are e/affected by education policy. It is, as noted in the Introduction, parallel to our interest in policy analysis (Webb and Gulson, 2015a).

For instance, we have briefly mentioned the colonial economics and racial geographies of the city as important events that may enact people. In this sense, the Africentric Alternative School provided accounts of people rather than people providing accounts of the school. There was a form of spatial fetishism, where the space of the intended school 'spoke' about people when people believed they were speaking about the school.

By extension, we note how ideas of *neoliberalism*, *biopolitics* and *non-/ representation* enact people and their respective accounts of the school. This book is not only about questions of epistemology, knowledge and reference. We are also interested in questions about policy ontologies, in the sense that ontology is: (a) enmeshed with people; (b) produced in varied time-spaces; (c) not anterior; (d) multiple; and (e) non-representational (for more see Webb and Gulson, 2015a: 22). We are focused specifically on policy enactments and the many ways these enactments are produced and appear coordinated (Ball et al., 2012).

In/compossibles

Deleuze (1993: 77) noted that events operate through 'compossibles' – things (bodies, states of affairs) compatible or possible in conjunction with another. As such, events are better understood as a multiplicity of compossibles rather than as a single, independent entity, or singularity.

Compossibles form and assemble into events. People may be involved as compossibles, but, for Deleuze, events are not caused by people, at least not as discrete actors. In fact, Deleuze would remark that people *become* events, whereas a series of compossibles produce a 'person-event'. The event of the Africentric Alternative School can be seen as a series of compossibles – colonial economics, the amalgamation of the Toronto District School Board (TDSB), Canadian multicultural policy, school choice policy, policy entrepreneurs, the racialised geographies of Toronto and so on. Thus, these specific compossibles are compatible and made possible in conjunction with each other. As an illustration, we perform some of the implicit compatibilities of these particular compossibles in the main body of the text.

Additionally, in this book we will introduce the idea of a 'dispositif' that functions similarly to compossibles. 'Dispositif' is a term that refers to different discourses, institutions, and knowledge structures (law, policy, architecture) that maintain the exercise and arrangements of power (Foucault, 1977). Hence, we are not 'using' compossibles as much as drawing and amalgamating a set of congruent ideas. Additionally, it may be the case that events are produced through 'incompossibles' – things not compatible or in disjunction with another (Deleuze, 1993: 81, in a critique of Leibniz's position).

Incompossible events are produced through bifurcations, divergences, discord and violence. The significance of incompossibles is the role that chance has in the production of events. In this sense, events have no goal, no determinate outcome. Even the most well-designed event – if that is possible – will produce unintended effects due to the role that chance has in the production of events; something congruent with ideas of policy as ad hoc and uncertain.

Moreover, a theory of events based entirely on compossibles is a theory that devolves quickly into a technical, rationalistic and conscious assemblage of compatible ideas – like putting together a puzzle that is already produced in ways that assume a completed product. Incompossibles, instead, produce events haphazardly and violently. The incompossibility of education policy, for example, is to invert its claim as a techno-rational instrument in the improvement of schooling, and to understand it as an instrument of incompleteness, indeterminacies, and ad hoc-ery. Education policy as an incompossible is quickly unmasked as an instrument of power, rather than the 'rational', 'neutral' and 'compromised' syntheses of ready-made compossibles.

It is also the case that what we discuss as in/compossibles of the Africentric Alternative School event are events in themselves, for instance the event of colonial economics or the event of the Yonge Street Riot. In this sense, events would appear to be infinite, and to some extent they are, both in number and in that events have no beginning and no end. Hence, this accounts for our suspicions of narratives and stories. The idea of a series, however, may be a better way to think about events in the way we are using the idea. As a series, events can be delimited by three conditions:

• space and time
• prehensions (affect)
• force and power

Condition 1: Space and time

First, events are characterised by the idea of *extension*, and specifically ideas of space and time. Understood as a series, events are delimited by the relationships they have to other events, wholes and parts, time and space. Events are marked by the passage of time, but in ways where the event is that 'which has just happened and that which is about to happen, but never that which is happening' (Deleuze, 1990a: 8).

Spatially, events are marked by the intensities produced within different in/compossibles that occur somewhere. Space provides the specific 'flavour' of intrinsic properties of the event, and time, oddly enough, the location of the event within the series of in/compossibles. As such, space is often conflated with place when intrinsic properties are understood as endemic or unique to a situation (rather than properties produced haphazardly through chance). Thus, the idea of space and time are not limits, but coordinates from which to identify events along a series (Deleuze, 1993: 77).

Amin and Thrift (2002: 30) noted that the:

> encounter, and the reaction to it, is a formative element in the urban world. So places, for example, are best thought of not so much as enduring sites but as moments of encounter, not so much as 'presents', fixed in space and time, but as variable events; twists and fluxes of interrelation.

This is the result of understanding time and space as unfixed, but rather, in extension with themselves as well.

Condition 2: Prehensions (affect)

Second, events are delimited by *prehensions* – 'the "datum" of another element that prehends it' and in turn 'anticipate psychic life' (Deleuze, 1993: 78). Prehensions are the attributes of events that mark them as significant in some way, and that designate them differently than, for example, an 'occurrence' or 'happening'.

Prehensions are those things that are not apprehended or understood (that is, not cognitive), but rather, prehensions produce enactments and form relationships between entities. Subsequently, prehensions can be interpreted into familiar ideas of 'feelings'.

31

However, the act of interpretation is an act that is often completed, in a matter of seconds, within the dominant social and cultural discourses at work. Thus, 'the event is inseparably the objectification of one prehension and the subjectification of another; it is at once public and private, potential and real, participating in the becoming of another event and the subject of its own becoming' (Deleuze, 1993: 78).

Prehensions orient and position subjects initially, but conclusively once they have been interpreted into emotions. For example, the Africentric Alternative School produced several prehensions, perhaps characterised as excitement or revulsion, and oriented people respectively. In this sense, prehensions are similar to other forms of embodied knowledge, for instance the idea of affect. This matters for understanding how policy works for, as Anderson (2014: 4) contends, contemporary governance, and this includes the work of policy, involves governance through affect, which has become 'an object-target for specific and multiple forms of power'.

Condition 3: Force and power

Third, events are the 'potential immanent within a particular confluence of forces' (Stagoll, 2010: 90). In this sense, not everything is an event. Instead, events are produced only in relation to a particular arrangement of forces, and only in relation to what is produced through this specific arrangement. While this condition appears somewhat tautological, the emphasis on power and force (and the unexpected result, or chance) is crucial to understanding events. To alleviate some of the perceived repetition in the third condition, rearranging forces would produce different events.

Events fluctuate between something immanent or virtual and something actual. Events are not the 'disruption of some continuous state, but rather the state is constituted by events "underlying it"' (Stagoll, 2010: 90). For example, the event of the Africentric Alternative School is not so much a combination of prior events but rather an intensity of force at a particular moment. It is thus that we write this book in a series of events rather than a chronology of events.

Our study of the becoming of the Africentric Alternative School identifies (a) the preconditions or the immanence for the school-becoming, in relation to (b) the specific ways that school actualised or became, and (c) the types of force used to move from immanence to actualisation. In this delicate process of becoming, the school's actualisation was influenced by several factors; factors that, if used differently (or if other factors were used), would have likely produced a different school and/or produced the school differently.

More importantly, our analysis identifies and attends to some of the possibilities that remained unrealised among the different preconditions of the school's becoming, and between the specific forces that actuated the school. In this sense, our analysis examines some of the unrealised possibilities left between various preconditions and the various forms of power that produced the school. Our goal in discussing some of the unrealised possibilities is designed to examine opportunities that are not readily observed, pursued or actuated, and to determine reasons for their exclusion. *Our methodological goals, then, are designed to develop new political possibilities.*

Eventalisation

Our methodological goals resonate with the practices of *eventalisation* coined by Michel Foucault (2000: 226). The attention we give to in/compossibles alters conceptions of events that rely on single causes or single triggers. Instead, we are interested in the multiplicity or plurality of causes, where:

> Causal multiplication consists in analysing and event according to the multiple presses that constitute it ... '[E]ventalization' thus works by constructing around the singular event analysed a process a 'polygon' or rather a 'polyhedron' of intelligibility, the number of whose faces is not given in advance and can never properly be taken as finite. (Foucault, 2000: 227)

As we noted, eventalisation is concerned with identifying and attributing the in/compossibles that remained unrealised or dormant. Thus, eventalisation identifies the 'connections, encounters, supports, blockages, plays of forces, strategies, and so on that at a given moment establish what subsequently comes to count a being self-evident, universal and necessary' (Foucault, 2000: 226–7).

Finally, our use of eventalisation is designed to provide accounts that have been displaced by other accounts that treat the phenomenon of the school's becoming as a matter of epistemology, knowledge and representation. Thus, eventalisation is a method that makes 'visible a *singularity* at places where there is a temptation to invoke historical constants, an immediate anthropological trait, or an obviousness that imposes itself uniformly on all' (Foucault, 2000: 226).

Eventalisation is how we place the becoming of the school within a series of contested histories; how we alter the 'heroic' tropes of those involved with education policy; and how we introduce a detailed sense of the complexities and indeterminacies involved in the school's becoming.

Not so feel-good

It would be much easier, and a lot safer, to adopt many of the accepted scientistic discourses around 'qualitative education research' and/or 'case study'. Such a position would allow us to zero in on the heroics of a few people who exercised their 'agency' in the face of the uncertainty and fear that has permeated the globe.

As White authors, adopting the more traditional scientistic discourse would highlight the incongruent epistemologies and differential power dynamics involved with our 'outsider' positions. More likely, adopting a scientistic discourse of qualitative research would highlight our interests in race but in ways that question our intentions to become 'allies', or perhaps read psychoanalytically as a kind of desirous fantasy to be with the Other. In the end, adopting a stance of qualitative research might allow us to be admitted to discourses of bravery, heroism or allies, but still mark us as ultimately naive, desirous, or flawed in some (or many) ways.

Our use of the event, conversely, is not an attempt to avoid such critiques of our work. The study of anti-Black racism by White researchers is rife with problems, and the possible critiques of our work listed above are all likely responses to this project. In addition to the possible responses to our work listed above, our intent to problematise race and problematise the associated politics designed around anti-racist practices is sure to elicit critiques of our work through the identifications of our own deep-seated racisms. For instance, one of interviewees decided that our attention to race is indicative of our own racist proclivities (racist from the outset).

Why problematise the very recourses available to redress and equity? Why not simply illustrate how the school became, and illustrate how to replicate this story elsewhere? Our problematising stance is designed to unsettle notions of contemporary racial politics, and to show the complexities and changing material conditions that now *use* racial politics and education policies in ways that perpetuate and continue unjust and unequal educational conditions.

TWO

Policy and biopolitics: the event of race-based statistics in Toronto

> I think … [the establishment of a Black-focused school] took so long because we're all very comfortable, and we've become very complacent in how we treat students in our schools, and more specifically, how we treat students of colour within our schools. It has been suggested time and time and time again, and we will have a shooting in a school, we will have a death in a school, and somebody else will recommend … [a Black-focused school], and everybody says, 'yeah, great idea! We really should deal with this because students', Black students' self-esteem is down a hole and we need to do something about it'. And we talk and we nod and we smile, and then we forget about it. (Weiss, 2010: film time 11.00–11.56)

There was momentum to introduce Black-focused schooling in Toronto in the early 1990s, assisted by the election of the social democratic New Democratic Party at the time. In 1991, a Black Secretariat was formed by the provincial government, and ideas about Black-focused schooling were proposed in 1992 by a multilevel Ontario government working group, the Four-level Government/African Canadian Community Working Group. As part of recommendations in their report *Towards a new beginning*, the working group proposed a targeted programme called 'Focussed School' to be implemented in schools that had high percentages of Black/African Canadian students in each of the cities making up Greater Toronto (Ontario Government/African Canadian Community Working Group, 1992).

The arguments for Black-focused schools in Toronto emphasised the need for a Black-oriented curriculum as an intervention into ongoing educational and social disadvantage for Black students. This meant arguing for curriculum change in existing public schools in addition to proposing separate 'Black-focused' schools (Dei, 1995; James, 2011). However, by the mid-1990s and early 2000s the idea of Black-focused schooling had entered a hiatus, with a decline in focus on racial issues brought about by a combination of a change in provincial government in 1995, with a Conservative government in power until 2003, and the dismantling of the Ontario Anti-Racism Secretariat by the incoming government, and the reorganisation of the Greater Toronto School District.

In the mid-2000s, there was renewed focus on Black-focused education in Toronto against a backdrop of continued Black student underachievement on standardised tests, large dropout rates, disproportionate rates of suspension and expulsion for Black students, and violence in schools (Thompson and Wallner, 2011; Dei and Kempf, 2013; Johnson, 2013). Two major proposals were introduced to remedy these conditions during this time. The first proposal was designed to develop a broad-based Black-focused curriculum model that would be piloted and eventually implemented across the entire district (Dei and Kempf, 2013: 67–8). The second proposal was designed to develop separate Black-focused schools – a proposal that became a lightning rod for public discourses about safety in schooling and that displaced the curriculum proposal. Both proposals emanated from debates, over the period of a year in the Toronto District School Board (TDSB), about the introduction of race-based data collection as the means to substantiate, and then ameliorate, endemic and systemic academic underachievement for Black students.

This chapter connects race-based statistics to race-based violence, ideas of counting and racial biopolitics. The focus is on two events. The first is a 2008 a report into school safety, the *Falconer report* (SCSAP, 2008), which urged the use of 'race-based statistics' in the TDSB and reignited the overall move towards Black-focused schooling. We connect this report, and its plea to use race-based statistics in discipline-related incidents in schooling to racial profiling and policing in Toronto in the early 2000s. The chapter concludes with the TDSB decision in 2004–5 to collect race-based statistics, as a second policy event that preceded the *Falconer report*.

The *Falconer report*: school violence and the call for race-based statistics

In August 2005, the Coalition of African Canadian Organizations (CACO) – a Toronto coalition of 22 Black community groups – was formed in response to gun murders in the city involving members of the Black community. The summer of 2005 was known colloquially as the 'summer of the gun', where 33 incidents, many fatal, occurred between late June and early August. While formed around these particular incidents, the CACO was also connected to over 15 years of advocacy for focus on violence against the Black community in Toronto. This advocacy included responses to police shootings of young Black men in the late 1980s and early 1990s (more on this in Chapter Five). In 2005, the CACO put forward an action plan to address the gun violence that had resulted in the murder of many Blacks in Toronto. The CACO would later morph into the African Canadian Coalition of Community Organizations, circa 2011–12, headed by Donna Harrow.

However, at 2.30 pm on 23 May 2007, less than two years after the CACO proposed action, a Black, male student, Jordan Manners, was fatally shot in the hallway of his school at C.W. Jefferys Collegiate Institute, in the Jane and Finch area of the city. This tragic event in the hallways of a school was the first time a student was shot and killed inside a Toronto school, and forced the TDSB to take immediate action. The board appointed a three-person School Community Safety Advisory Panel (SCSAP) in June 2007, with the goal of understanding the events leading up to Manners' tragic death. The panel was chaired by Julian Falconer, who had previously been counsel for the Urban Alliance on Race Relations. The terms of reference focused on practices and procedures at C.W. Jefferys regarding safety and discipline, and included a remit to seek input from the broader educational community.

On 10 January 2008 the panel tabled its report, vernacularly known as the *Falconer report*. The report criticised narrow views on what constituted 'school safety', notably views primarily concerned with security measures such as discipline and building security. Alternatively, the panel proposed that school safety issues should be reconsidered in light of what it identified as 'dysfunctional' learning environments. Specifically, 'school safety' should be synonymous with what the panel termed 'school health' and 'healthy learning environments' (SCSAP, 2008: 1–2).

The report proposed that the TDSB adopt strategies that would re-engage marginalised and 'complex-needs' students, by combining social services support with an inclusive curriculum. Underlying these ideas was a philosophy that was:

> engendered in the notion of equity, which has, as its most fundamental tenet, the recognition that people's differences are to be recognized and accounted for with a view to creating environments that do not push people out. Strategies geared towards inclusion involve adopting approaches and programs meant to recognize

and acknowledge the diversity of the student population. (SCSAP, 2008: 7)

As part of the recommendations of the report, the panel noted that many of the submissions to the panel called for race and disability to be included in the collection of statistics on expulsions and suspensions.★ It was clear that Black parents and community advocates felt that the policies of the TDSB around suspension and exclusions were disproportionately focused on Black students. The panel noted:

> parents asked that expulsion and suspension data be made available to the public by schools in a manner that provides for privacy issues and Freedom of Information. In the words of one parent, 'If we are sending our kids to your school, we have the right to get those statistics.' (SCSAP, 2008: 194)

Against this backdrop of both a request for the collection and distribution of statistics, relating to not only disciplinary but also identity categories, the panel concluded that previous policy directions in the TDSB had disproportionately affected 'students from racialized and marginalized communities'. However the report pleaded that evidence and data were needed to make policy decisions: 'Without statistics on race it is impossible to know … with any certainty, allowing an unfair discrediting of these communities [sic] concerns' (SCSAP, 2008: 194).

In 2004, the Ontario Human Rights Commission had recommended the collection of race-based statistics. The *Falconer report* followed this recommendation with Recommendation 8.1 that included:

a   that TDSB administration be directed to collect and analyze data on expulsions and suspensions … in order to monitor, prevent and combat any discriminatory effect on individuals … including students from racialized communities and students with disabilities …

b   that a researcher/statistician be designated to design an appropriate collection vehicle and data base to facilitate the collection and analysis of these statistics …

c   that the results become part of the school improvement process at both the Board and school level. (SCSAP, 2008: 194)

The 2004 recommendation by the Ontario Human Rights Commission was a result of much advocacy and contention around race-based statistics in Toronto, especially in the early 2000s. The recommendation by the *Falconer report* for race-based statistics on expulsions and suspensions was an extension of the type of race-based data collection that had been part of series of debates both in the city of Toronto around policing, and in the TDSB over the period of 2004 into 2005. We discuss these two debates about policing and education in the following sections.

Race-based statistics in Toronto: policy and profiling

The focus on expulsions and suspensions and race-based statistics, recommended in the *Falconer report*, came six years after the use of race-based statistics in raising questions about racial profiling in policing in Toronto. The issue of racial profiling was the central narrative in a series of reports about policing and race in the Toronto newspaper *The Toronto Star* beginning on 19 October 2002. The newspaper examined two years of arrest and charge data, via a freedom of information request, that included more than 480,000 incidents of individual arrest, and 800,000 charges laid by police between 1996 and 2002 (Henry and Tator, 2005). The *Star* concluded that, in Toronto, 'analysis of the crime data revealed significant disparities in the ways in which Blacks and Whites are treated in law enforcement practices' (Henry and Tator, 2005: 2).

Henry and Tator (2005), in an analysis of the *Star's* reporting and the police and public reaction to the reporting, concluded that the controversy about race-based statistics and policy pointed to the paradox of Canada's approach to race and equality. Namely, that while there is a belief in the principles of fairness, justice and equality, this is countered by 'a huge body of evidence to suggest that racial bias and discrimination in all of its continually mutating forms is deeply embedded in the very fabric of Canadian culture' (Henry and Tator, 2005: 112–13). Henry and Tator (2005) concluded that what the *Star* report showed was that the repudiation, or outright denial, of racism by the Conservative provincial government, and the government's elimination of anti-racism policies and programs provided 'fertile ground' for the incidence of racial profiling (2005: 108).

The database that the *Star's* reports used was the only one in Toronto, at that time, that used race-based statistics. However, it was a precursor to others as the connection of racial profiling to race-based statistics became the focal point of debates about the role of race-based data collection in other arenas. For example, Dei and Kempf argued that:

> Racial profiling has been a controversial and important legal and social issue in the Canadian context ... Race-based statistics [RBS] have been crucial to highlighting and thus challenging these practices. In the case of two of Canada's largest police forces, those of Toronto and Kingston, RBS was used to 'uncover' the presence of racial profiling. (Dei and Kempf, 2005: 6)

It was this idea of 'uncovering' an invisible presence that was part of the push for race-based statistics within the TDSB.

Race-based statistics and the TDSB

While the *Falconer report* was based around expulsions and suspensions, the general principle of collecting race-based statistics connected to schooling practices had already been introduced in the TDSB in 2005, with surveys of students in 2006, and parents in 2008. These surveys included race-based identifiers, with the aim of correlating demographic data with student achievement. The introduction of these surveys occurred after the Harris Conservative government eliminated the Black Secretariat, and equity concerns and anti-racism initiatives disappeared from the policy agenda and the official rhetoric. Brown (2005b) argued that the only time Toronto schools actually tracked performance by race was during the 1970s and 1980s, when a large percentage of Black students were placed in courses that did not prepare them for university, and in 1991, when the former Board of Education of the City of Toronto surveyed students and concluded that Black students dropped out at a higher rate than students of other racialised and ethnic backgrounds.

In 2004 the TDSB was only gathering student success indicators, which correlated student performance with place of birth. The statistics showed the number of credits teenagers had earned by the end of grade ten – if students did not have 16 credits or more by this time they were considered 'at risk' of graduating late or not at all – according to their country of origin. In relation to this collection of information, Robinson (2007) stated that, 'other than numbers pointing out how many students [were not] graduating from a specific geographical region, there [were not] any race-based statistics to show there [was] a large number of black youth dropping out of school'.

The absence of race-based statistics was used both as a support for, and opposition to, the idea there was a correlation between race and achievement. The absence of race-based statistics further obfuscated discussions about whether there should be a focus on particular types of education for different demographic groups. Amanda Alvaro, the provincial Ministry of Education's spokesperson argued, 'at this time there are few statistics to suggest academic achievement is based on race or ethnicity' (Kalinowski and Brown, 2005). The idea of 'evidence', and providing new 'evidence' for educational achievement became central to arguments about introduction of race-based data collection.

The push to introduce race-based statistics

Despite the lack of support for race-based statistics from the Conservative Ontario government, there was support for race-based statistics within the TDSB, and for efforts to broaden the demographic data collected about students, and to connect these data to student achievement. In a regular meeting of the TDSB on 20 October 2004, following the report of the Program and School Services Committee (which met on 12 October 2004), a motion was put forward targeted at secondary school students. The decision of the board was that the TDSB staff, under the aegis of the Program and School Services Committee, and in consultation with the Ontario Human Rights Commission, would: 'develop a research program that examines student achievement in the TDSB including such factors as gender, race, ethnicity, mother tongue, income of place of residence' (TDSB, 2004b: 709). This motion represented the beginning of what would become a year of activity and advocacy throughout the board around race-based statistics.

At the next TDSB board meeting on 17 November, some Trustees attempted to derail the proposed research programme. Rather than develop a programme, some Trustees proposed that a survey of community and staff should be carried out to see if the statistics and programme were needed. The amendment read that first the TDSB should undertake a survey of schools, the communities and staff to ascertain whether the race-based statistics were wanted. The amendment read that:

> our community and staff [should] ... be surveyed to see whether or not a statistically sufficient number of people wish to be categorized in this way, and that full consideration be given to how we are defining race, how

we will compile these statistics, how they will be reported and what uses these statistics are meant to support, and that a full report on these questions come back to the Board before any race statistics are gathered in any way, shape or form. (TDSB, 2004c: 794–5)

What is evident in this amendment is the ways in which debates about race-based statistics continued to be contested, and the concerns about how the statistics might be used. As Dei, a professor at the Ontario Institute for Studies in Education at the University of Toronto, suggested, some people were simply against reinstating the collection of race-based statistics because they feared this data would 'reinforce negative stereotypes, ignore or address low student performance or simply blame individual educators' (2005: np).

The proposed amendment was defeated, and the trustees who proposed the amendment then became satirical about identity categories, with a proposed quasi- or *faux* amendment that read that the board should support a motion: 'to also gather statistics on being fat, gay, ugly, "geeky," Jewish, Muslim, fundamentalist and a turban-wearing Sikh' after 'income and place of residence' (TDSB, 2004c: 794).

In response to the *faux* motion, two trustees proposed to directly set the parameters of collection, including that the board should repudiate deficit readings of populations in relation to identity and achievement. The amendments proposed were:

> (b1) That staff in consultation with the Ontario Human Rights Commission and educational experts develop research proposals that identify the factors within the school system which may inhibit student achievement. Such factors should include, but not be limited to, differences in gender, race, ethnicity, mother tongue, income and place of residence;
>
> (b2) That in undertaking such a research proposal, the Board reaffirm the long established fact that there is no correlation between these factors and the inherent capacity of students to learn and achieve success, and that the results of such research and its ensuing recommendations be used to assist the Board in implementing strategies to help all students achieve their fullest potential for success in our schools … (TDSB, 2004c: 795)

These amendments were carried. However, it took a year, that is until the 14 December 2005 meeting, for this to be incorporated into what was known as the *Closing the achievement gap* report authored by the Program and School Services Committee.

Closing the achievement gap report, 14 December 2005

Race-based statistics returned to the TDSB with the *Closing the achievement gap* report, presented to the TDSB at the 14 December 2005 meeting. The report outlined that the TDSB collected 'student demographic data on age, gender, country of birth, mother tongue, language spoken at home, and place of residence'. What the report reiterated, and this reinforced the decision taken by the TDSB in November 2004, was that the board did not collect data on either race or ethnic background, or on socioeconomic status. The report outlined that during 2003–4 and 2004–5 there had been much discussion and debate about the 'needs of students at-risk and students from racial and ethnocultural groups' (TDSB, 2005b: 1384). The report identified that, combined with the focus on school violence and safety, media reports had looked at school 'failure' by especially 'Black Caribbean' students. The report highlighted that there had been over 20 years of community advocacy about 'the achievement gap between students of racialized communities and other students' (TDSB, 2005b: 1385). The report noted that:

> Since the early 1980's, community groups in the city of Toronto from the African Canadian community, the Portuguese Canadian community, and umbrella groups speaking on behalf of newcomer/ESL groups began to identify barriers related to differences in race and culture with the school system. (TDSB, 2005b: 1385)

In making the recommendation to survey students for the purposes of race-based data collection, the report outlined that following the 17 November 2004 meeting there were questions from the board:

a Is race and ethnicity a credible factor for data collection?

b Is there a positive educational and social purpose that can be served by the collection of such data?

c Is the collection of data legally permitted?

d Since the collection of data on race and ethnicity is a voluntary process to be done through self-identification, how can the TDSB best build commitment to its implementation, so that data is complete and useful. (TDSB, 2005b: 1379–80)

The responses of the Program and School Services Committee to questions 1 and 2 provided an interesting insight into the state of debate in Toronto around race-based statistics. The response identified that while race and ethnicity are social rather than scientific categories, these categories are important for self-identification – that 'most individuals and groups appear to have, among their range or identities, some notion of racial or ethnic identity' (TDSB, 2005b: 1380), and that: 'the historic social cleavages that result from perceptions of different treatment of groups based on race and ethnicity also confirm the existence of race and ethnicity as factors to be considered in social policy' (TDSB, 2005b: 1380).

The report directly addressed issues of profiling and stereotyping, highlighting that while the *Toronto Star* report had used profiling as a way of highlighting how police actions disproportionately targeted Black Torontonians, that the collection of race-based statistics in education would not lead to negative effects. The report stated that:

> there is no current evidence that the collection of race and ethnic data on the TDSB student population leads to racial stereotyping or profiling or of negative stigmatizing of schools. The collection of race data by Statistics Canada, which is used to inform social policy, has not itself caused a rise in racism or racial stereotyping among the Canadian public. (TDSB, 2005b: 1380)

The TDSB report is in accord with a paper by George Sefa Dei and Arlo Kempf, based on a paper in support of race-based statistics that Dei presented to the Canadian Race-Relations Foundation Policy Dialogue in October 2005. George Sefa Dei played an interesting role in this debate, both as an intellectual contributor, creating concepts and arguments to frame the debate, and participating in the political arena. In the dialogue paper, the arguments that Dei and Kempf made were reflected in some of the responses in the advisory committee report. Dei and Kempf contended: '[t]he collection of statistics is not only useful but also necessary in order to determine whether people of various racial backgrounds are being treated equitably by the system' (2005:

11). Dei and Kempf's response seemed to be that there are already problems anyway, and that labelling and stereotyping might occur. They stated: '[t]he truth of the matter however, is that statistics neither stigmatise nor label minority communities any more so than they are already have been [sic] by segments of the larger society' (2005: 17).

The TDSB report included broader recommendations for pedagogical opportunities to talk about race and ethnicity with students in the TDSB. In discussing the implementation issues, the report identified that self-identification by students and parents 'may produce feelings of discomfort' (TDSB, 2005b: 1391), and as such:

> For these reasons, staff recommends that a data collection process which requires students to self identify by race or ethnicity must be preceded by opportunities for informed school or classroom learning about and appreciation for the racial and ethnic diversity of the City's population. Staff will produce a brief curriculum document on the topic of racial or ethnic diversity, which can be adapted by teachers for classroom description. (TDSB, 2005b: 1391)

The report asserted that there would be positive educational and social purposes for the collection of race and ethnic data, including assessing the effectiveness of programmes for specific students, supporting planning and resourcing, and supporting interventions to overcome 'systemic barriers to achievement' (TDSB, 2005b: 1381). In 2006 and 2008 the surveys were introduced:

> In 2006, TDSB students in Grades 7 to 12 and in 2008, parents of Kindergarten to Grade 6 students were invited for the first time to participate in a system-wide Census. Together, the two Censuses have provided the Board with a valuable source of information on its diverse student population, including their demographics, family background, self perceptions and in- and out-of-school experiences. (TDSB, nd)

Summary

In this chapter we have looked at the way the *Falconer report* reinvigorated a focus on race-based statistics around issues of exclusion and suspension, and therefore indirectly connected to educational achievement for Black students. The report was identified as an important event in the creation of the Alternative School in that it followed initial discussions in 2008 about an alternative school. On 27 June 2007, the board voted for 'staff [to] present a report on the feasibility of a pilot Afrocentric alternative school including examples and information on of Afrocentric schools in other school boards' (TDSB, 2007a: 719; see Chapter Three for more details).

The release of the *Falconer report* followed the request for an Africentric school, but the crucial meeting at the TDSB to decide on the establishment of the school came less than a month after the report's release. Thompson and Wallner (2011), hence, contend that the death of Jordan Manners provided what they call, somewhat perversely, a 'window of opportunity' for the TDSB to initiate Afrocentric schooling provision. This decision followed what had been close to a decade of linking violence, racial profiling and race-based statistics.

Race-based statistics formed an important component of reinvigorated debates about Black-focused in schooling in Toronto. The focus on achievement was reinforced by recommendations from the board's advisory committee on student achievement, and was again reinforced by Dei and Kempf who stated that:

> RBS in education is not meant to stigmatise or celebrate certain bodies to the benefit or exclusion of others, but rather to identify the ways in which the educational systems are succeeding or failing in their task of delivering equitable education. Race-based statistics should look at student, teacher and administration achievement alongside qualitative and quantitative analysis of race within curricula, teacher training and hiring at all levels. (2005: 9)

According to Lloyd McKell (2005) – the TDSB Central Coordinator for Parent and Community before he was appointed as the Executive Officer for Student and Community in 31 August 2005 – the persistently high record of Black student underachievement and dropout rates in the system was a concern for the board, which regarded this 'as a matter of great urgency' (2005: 4). In his view, this sense of urgency was sparked by public discussions and reports around Black students' performance in the school system. This was key for Dei and Kempf, who contended that: 'The time is now for race-based statistics. In the context of education the whole debate is around the failure of schools to educate Black and African-Canadian youth, as well as the call for African-centred schools' (Dei and Kempf, 2005: 25). For Dei, the hope was that race-based statistics would replace stereotypes with 'fact', and for the TDSB that these statistics would frame future discussions about schooling.

Biopolitics and accounting for ourselves in numbers

*The debate about race-based statistics in Toronto constituted a politics of educational recognition via the imbrication of calculation with governance. There was an evident tension between the kinds of racism that were not 'accounted' for, and how raciologies were practised and perpetuated in education as part of anti-racist attempts.

Counting the bodies: census- and race-based statistics

The creation of statistical data based on race and ethnicity by the state, and its various levels of government, is the focus for critique and debate in the social sciences. Kukutai and Thompson (2015: 41) contended that 'counting and classifying people is seen first and foremost as a political endeavor'. The creation of differentiation becomes necessary, for as Hacking (2016: 66) noted: '[e]numeration demands *kinds* of things or people to count. Counting is hungry for categories.' Within the technology of counting, categories are imbued with power and imaginaries (Simon and Piché, 2012), and there is, as Rose (1999b: 98) posited, a co-constitutive function to numbers and politics, where 'it is not just that the domain of numbers is politically composed, but also that the domain of politics is made up numerically'.

The politics of numbers has been 'top down' with the classification by the state connected to 'an extension of hierarchical arrangements and dominant group interests' (Kukatai and Thompson, 2015: 41), and 'bottom up', where in countries identified or self-identified as multicultural, 'ethnic minorities have successfully lobbied to have ethnic distinctions recognised in official data collections' (Kukutai and Thompson, 2015: 41). Evident in most cases, and this holds for the focus on race-based statistics, is that globally 'much of the diverse nomenclature used to describe collective identities (for example, ethnicity, race, ancestry, and indigeneity) is underpinned by the common concept of descent' (Kukutai and Thompson, 2015: 42, citing Morning, 2008).

The idea of focusing on race in multicultural countries like Canada highlights the disputes over whether difference is filtered through biology. While contemporary discussions in Canada are fraught over whether race should be a premise for classification, race is a part of the history of counting in the country. The early census 'between 1871 and 1941 [was] classified according to race, in which race served as salient boundaries, distinguishing socially defined group of the head, stature, colour of skin, etc.' (Thompson, 2012: 1411). These references were replaced after the Second World War by 'ethnicity', and the contemporary term is 'visible minorities' (Thompson, 2012).

The paradox of counting

Hacking asks 'why there is such a pervasive tendency to apply the category of race' (2005: 104). His response is that it is very difficult to escape the clutches of race and race science – the relationship to empire, to control, to the pervasive and at times seductive idea that once we classify using racial categories we are denoting that the different classes are 'essentially different types of people' (Hacking, 2005: 104). Hence, the creation of race-based statistics is a double-edged sword. As Bonnett and Carrington (2000: 487) outlined, 'it seems self-evident that a necessary component of creating more inclusive institutions is the availability of more comprehensive information on racial and ethnic differences', yet conversely and simultaneously, the 'very process of compelling people to assign themselves to one of a small number of racial and ethnic "boxes" is, at best, essentialist and, at worst, racist' (Bonnett and Carrington, 2000: 487–8).

In Toronto there was a focus on police and racial profiling, and advocacy around demography and education. In other countries, such as England, access to higher education and workplace equality have been the target areas for debates about the collection of race- and ethnicity-based statistics. Bonnett and Carrington (2000) posited that there is a 'disabling paradox' (2000: 487) to the collection of these statistics that comprises 'political tensions between an authoritarian aspect of social surveillance and control and an egalitarian principle of redistribution and open, transparent management' (2000: 488). Advocates traversed the terrain of ethics and political pragmatism, or the 'problematic necessity' (Bonnett and Carrington, 2000) that characterises debates and practices of enumeration. It is the paradox of enumeration that advocates in Toronto attempted to circumvent in arguments for race-based statistics. Simon and Piché asked: '[d] oes distinguishing and characterizing populations according to their ethnic origins constitute a risk of stigmatization or is it, on the contrary, an asset for measuring and explaining discrimination and for demanding more inclusive policies?' (2012: 1358).

For Dei and Kempf (2005: 16), the argument was that '[w]e need ... [race based statistics] in order to establish a much needed degree of accountability'. In

Canada, the lineage of race-based statistics has been framed as a social justice move, such as the inclusion of 'mixed race' categories in the 1996 census. This enabled the 'uncomfortable' category of race to be framed around equality and fairness, and, hence, 'made it possible for the multicultural nation-building project to be reimagined in multiracial terms' (Thompson, 2012: 1421). For those arguing for race-based statistics in Toronto, the categories provided a way 'to pinpoint and measure the material manifestations of racism in Canada. Such statistics are an important element of any project which aims to combat racism' (African Canadian Legal Clinic, 2008: 1).

Policy events like the debates about race-based statistics can be located as part of the enduring nature of racial legacies and racial biopolitics. As Amin maintained: '[c]ontinuity is secured through a machinery of human ordering in different domains of social life, maintained through state rules and regulations, social codes and conventions, myths of heritage and community, technologies of human governance' (Amin, 2010: 6).

The machinery of ordering – particularly the combination of political knowledge with disciplines such as demography and statistics – has been key to the examination of processes of life and death at the level of populations (Lemke, 2011: 5). In looking at counting and statistics in Toronto, a notion of biopolitics that is useful looks: 'to embrace all the specific strategies and contestations over problematizations of collective human vitality, morbidity and mortality; over the forms of knowledge, regimes of authority and practices of intervention that are desirable, legitimate and efficacious' (Rabinow and Rose, 2006: 197). Policy has a crucial role in biopolitics (Lather, 2006), especially when, as Harney and Moten suggested, it is about 'correction', where '[t]his is the first rule of policy. It fixes others' (2013: 78).

We suggest that this 'fixing' can be part of the new normality of racial biopolitics (Amin, 2010). Amin proposes that racial biopolitics involves the ways in which '[b]odily traits and "ethnic" cultures are becoming the basis upon which peoples are allocated rights, identities, a place in the world ... at the expense of other modes of marking community and negotiating difference' (Amin, 2010: 10). The legitimacy of the Africentric Alternative School as part of the alternative school programme in Toronto was not only to do with who gets to establish a school of choice, but also about what types of bodily traits were conflated with what knowledge counts, and who is able to do this counting. As Gillborn noted, 'statistical methods themselves encode particular assumptions which, in societies that are structured in racial domination, often carry biases that are likely to further discriminate against particular minoritized groups' (2010: 254).

Clough and Willse (2011) noted that the use of statistics is part of the abstraction of the biological, or those categories that continue to bear connections to the biological such as race. They posit that '[t]he calculation of biological differences enables a process of value production in the differences of race, or in the differences of life capacities rendered as racial probabilities to be circulated as data' (Clough and Willse, 2011: 51).

The argument is that data such as statistics brings the assessment of the future into a representation of the present, and 'in so doing generates and circulates value, or what might better be called the biovalue of risk or life and death chances' (Clough and Willse, 2011: 51). It is this idea of value that Dei pointed to in arguing that race-based statistics are crucial and interconnected around power and bodies, such that '[w]e can only address the issue of different bodies in our schools ... if we are prepared to work with certain statistics that speak about certain absences (2008: 357–8). Hence, the idea of 'counting' has two interconnected meanings: recognising (or accounting) and value (or worth).

Evidence and policy

Race-based statistics provide a solution to the requirement for more compelling evidence. Race-based statistics, used as, and to, legitimate forms of classification, depend on the rationality of policy sciences – where infallibility of evidence is required for such policies' application, through statistics as exactness; or, in other words, and in relation to the above discussion: (a) an insistence on biological governance through the infallibility of statistics, (b) an exacting correction or fixing of deficits, and (c) precise statements about collective and individual recognition and worth. Hence, for Dei and Kempf the issue was a new form of policy 'persuasion', in which '[a]t the social level, such statistics offer us information relating to the exact nature of the problem with which we are faced' (2005: 16).

This is governance by, and of, the complexity and reductionism of numbers. Nonetheless, the positing of race-based statistics as a necessary form of evidence is part of the political nature of numbers and the ways in which a population is managed – but paradoxically, 'whilst numbers seem indispensable to politics, they also appear to depoliticize whole areas of political judgement' (Rose, 1999b: 198). In so doing, the depoliticisation of political judgement requires the politically marginalised to *account for themselves*, and to do so in the statistical registers already used by the prevailing policy practices of biological regulation, deficit correction and recognitions of worth. Thus, the depoliticisation of political judgement or, conversely, the appeals to 'exacting' and 'objective' numbers, fall upon those without political resources and, hence, maintain forms of biopolitical governance in ways that persuade those without political capital to argue they should be counted, and to account for themselves, within registers and categories already defined and used to regulate life. Not to do so amounts to taking risks with one's life and, as a result, completely precludes 'other modes of marking community and negotiating difference' (Amin, 2010: 10).

As a result, the depoliticisation of political judgement through numbers is about forms of authority. The argument for a focus on Black underachievement was lacking an authority in the calculation practices of the Toronto District School Board (TDSB), as the number was absent. As a result, arguments that underachievement was part of racism were dismissed. If a political position is given authority there is no need for numbers, but when authority is in doubt, there is a search for objectivity. As Rose noted:

> where mistrust of authority flourishes, where experts are the target of suspicion and their claims are greeted with scepticism by politicians, disputed by professional rivals, distrusted by public opinion, where decisions are contested and discretion is criticized, the allure of numbers increases. It in these circumstances that professionals and experts try to justify their judgements on the ground of objectivity, and frequently frame this objectivity in numerical form. Numbers are resorted to in order to settle or diminish conflicts in a contested space of weak authority. (Rose, 1999b: 208)

This is as much the case for anti-racist positions as for those that are part of the maintenance of White supremacy. The reduction to objectivity has the same allure of authority.

THREE

The (micro)politics of racial neoliberalism

with Viviana Pitton

This chapter maps the event of the alternative school policy of the Toronto District School Board (TDSB). The focus of this chapter is to map neoliberalism, and specifically racial neoliberalism, onto the city of Toronto. To accomplish what we might call this policy cartography (Webb and Gulson, 2013), the chapter traces the policy development of the Africentric Alternative School within the TDSB to identify how the school's development moved between different spaces and between different times.

Our tracing of a specific instance of neoliberalised policy is placed in relation to broader attempts to develop racial equity in schooling.* In other words, this chapter traces 'local' and micropolitical instances of the board's alternative school policy *in relation* to 'global' and macropolitical influences of educational and racial neoliberalism. This 'fluid' analysis looks at how power and force operate within educational equity attempts and illustrates the necessary but, ultimately, insufficient attempts at educational equity that rely solely on moral and epistemological, including statistical, arguments.

As such, this chapter does not explicate the epistemological influences or knowledge claims influencing the event of the school's becoming; instead, this chapter aims to explore material and ontological aspects of the policy environment affecting the event. The spatial and temporal analysis of this chapter underscores how objects and subjects easily interchange positions depending on the location of the analysis. As such, this chapter maps (1) how policy 'activists' simultaneously are policy 'subjects'; (2) how school mission statements are simultaneously efforts to develop a brand within educational quasi-markets; (3) how discourses of parental choice are conflated into contradictory discourses of educational entrepreneurialism and equity; and (4) how moral statements against racism are erased through pressures to maintain the dominant policies and practices of colour-blind (neoliberal) multiculturalism.

Toronto's fertile neoliberal educational environment

The *Toronto Star* reported that Angela Wilson learned about the TDSB's alternative school policy in 2003 while participating in an education forum in Etobicoke, a western borough of Toronto. According to the *Star*, Wilson was surprised to learn that the board encouraged parents to establish alternative schools (*Toronto Star*, 18 November 2007).

Although a year would pass before she would obtain a copy of the dormant policy, Wilson continued a series of critiques about the education her children received in Etobicoke. She believed that a pattern existed in which Black students were being treated differently, receiving what she described as 'a ghetto education'. In her words, she did not 'sit back and let them run their school and not question things', and it did not take long for her to become 'well-known at 5050 Yonge', the location of the TDSB headquarters (Diebel, 2008).

As mentioned in the opening chapter, alternative schools in Toronto can be proposed and established by parents and community members, and are usually schools within existing schools. Parental choice is the primary driver of any alternative school, and is buttressed by provincial policy in Canada and then modified at school board level. However, education markets were not the original impetus for alternative schools. The provision of 'alternative' schools in Toronto emerged as part of a broader movement in the 1960s and 1970s around 'free schools', cooperative parent–teacher elementary schools, and community, conservative elementary schools (Levin, 1979). In the 1980s, alternative schools in Toronto were developed by different parent, language and cultural groups to control, and make more culturally relevant, their children's schooling, as challenges to 'an Anglocentric, Protestant [Eurocentric] and bourgeois regime' (Delhi, 1996: 78).

Alternative school policies were the purview of the old Toronto School Board prior to its amalgamation in 1998 with five other boards (York, East York, North York, Scarborough, Etobicoke). After amalgamation, the alternative schools programme went into hiatus during the 1990s and early 2000s.

Alternative and choice schools in Toronto: a long history for non-racialised groups

It is not clear from the *Toronto Star* article what document or policy Wilson received circa 2003, or from whom. It may have been a singular policy about alternative schools from one of the previous boards, or a kind of patchwork document that was created from the amalgamation. Nevertheless, Wilson and Donna Harrow would meet with Dave Reed (director of the TDSB) in May 2004. At that meeting, they discussed the possibility of creating a new school to remedy the underachievement of Black students in Toronto (*Toronto Star*, 18 November 2007).

The particular document that Wilson received in 2003 would have provided advice about establishing an alternative school under the auspices of the old Toronto board. A new TDSB policy would be ratified in three years future at the 27 June 2007 TDSB meeting (this was P062; see TDSB, 2007b). Regardless, the document Wilson received would powerfully stir the imaginations about an Africentric Alternative School.

At a regular meeting of the board on 23 June 2004, trustees brought forth recommendations from the Pathways to Success Committee (PSC). The PSC, which held its first meeting on 13 May 2004, identified various barriers that inhibited academic success for many students. The PSC's recommendations noted that students from identifiable racialised groups had significantly lower academic performance than that of their White counterparts. Furthermore, non-White racialised groups were at higher risk of dropping out of school.

Towards the end of the regular meeting, Trustee Payne made a motion to have the PSC:

> explore the idea of an innovative pilot school program in an urban inner-city area for at-risk students in general, and African Canadian students in particular, and inspect the research linking academic achievement of at-risk children, specifically those of African heritage, with cultural intervention and prevention programs. (TDSB, 2004a: 462)

Education policies supporting choice had been an ad hoc part of the Toronto school landscape for nearly 25 years when Trustee Payne put forward her motion. Private religious schools were a staple of the Toronto educational market for years. A First Nations school was established in 1977. Public choice schools in Toronto had been established in areas of gender (single-sex schools) and sexuality (gay and lesbian schools and the Pink Triangle Program, focused on Gay and Lesbian students). Choice within the public system was, therefore, a viable site of struggle for parents and advocates of different educational approaches.

The outcome of these contests, in the 2000s, was the 'public alternative programme model' in Toronto that was revived in 2004. In fact, on 20 October 2004 the TDSB minutes of the regular meeting stated under the heading 'Alternative Schools and Programs' that:

> The Board has many Alternative Schools and Programs that have different models for service delivery. It is highly recommended that we begin a detailed review of Alternative Schools and Programs with the goal of expanding options and models in the future. The Board has the people, programs and resources to provide the variety of options that parents demand. (TDSB, 2004b: 741)

Race, however, was a social marker that was conspicuously absent from any alternative school in Toronto at this time.

The event of proposing a Black-focused school

On 2 February 2005, the forum 'Making the grade: Are we failing our Black youth?' was held (and televised) to a standing-room only crowd of 500 people at the St Lawrence Centre in downtown Toronto. Numerous students, parents and community members stood outside, disappointed at being denied entry to the centre that evening.

Professor George Sefa Dei was one of several panellists asked to address the forum question. He asked and answered: 'Are we failing Black youth? Yes, yes, yes. The curriculum doesn't reflect their lives; there are too few Black teachers and the zero-tolerance policies stigmatize them. The drop-out rates don't tell the whole story: Black students are being pushed out' (Brown, 2005a). Dei re-proposed the idea – put forward 13 years earlier by the Four-level Government/ African Canadian Community Working Group and Ontario's Royal Commission on Learning (discussed in more detail in Chapter Five) – that school boards ought to establish Black-focused schools in attempts to remedy the low achievement and high dropout rates among Black students. In Dei's view, Black-focused schools would ensure Black youth an equal opportunity of success.

Dei continued his discussion by anticipating fairly routine criticisms to his re-proposal. He asserted 'these schools [Black-focused] would be very different from the segregated schools of the [United States] South, because those were designed to disconnect Blacks. These would be created to address a problem, and they would be open to students of any colour' (Brown, 2005a). Dei would elaborate on his points. He stated: 'there is a meaningful difference between forced segregation and separation. Segregationists in the first half of the 20th century sought to exclude Blacks from meaningful participation in society. By contrast, Black-focused schools aim to address an educational crisis and help minority youth succeed' (Dei, 2005). That is, this would be segregation for the purpose of inclusion rather than exclusion.

Dei continued his re-proposal, by negotiating publicly. He asserted: 'four Black-focused schools across Toronto [would be necessary], but [I'll] take one as an experiment' (Brennan and Brown, 2005). He proposed that the school would include more than 'teaching about Africa and slavery'; he wanted to see 'an experimental pilot project school with more Black teachers that [focused] on Black achievement and culture and Black contributions to society that sends students out into the world well-affirmed on who they are' (Brennan and Brown, 2005). In his view, a Black-focused school would benefit those students who were most at risk of failure, and the successes and best practices of the pilot school would be incorporated into the mainstream system.

Black-focused schools had been debated by the African Canadian community for many decades prior to Dei's proposal. There were Black-focused schools in Nova Scotia and New Brunswick. Canadian Black-focused schools could also draw a lineage going back to community-based or Black supplementary school movements in the UK (Gerrard, 2013) and the notion of independent Black institutions in the United States, with examples at various times in Ohio, Missouri, Washington, Wisconsin and California (Shujaa, 1988, 1992).

The response to Dei's suggestions ranged from enthusiasm to caution and disgust. Other panellists supported Dei's proposal and argued it was time to experiment with Black-focused schools. Many of the 500 attendees applauded the suggestions as well. However, former lieutenant governor Lincoln Alexander, the first Black member of the Canadian federal parliament – who, among other distinctions, had an award for promoting racial harmony named after him – was severely critical. He asserted:

> If you don't have a Black boss in the police department, does that mean you can't be a policeman? If you don't have a Black person as head of the law society, does that mean that you can't get a law degree? [...] These university professors ought to get out of their classrooms and see what's going on. (Kalinowski and Brown, 2005)

Similarly, other activists rejected the proposal. Zanana Akande, president of the Urban Alliance on Race Relations, argued that schools should reflect Canada's diversity, not fragment it. In Akande's view, 'schools should serve the population that's out there' and prepare it to live in an integrated society (Kalinowski and Brown, 2005). She supported the idea of running a temporary Black-focused school as a research project to assess the influence of Black teachers and a Black curriculum on student achievement, 'but not as a general program' (Kalinowski and Brown, 2005). For Akande, it was important to integrate Black history into the curriculum.

Akande's comments reflect a general confusion about what Dei meant with regard to his statements about a 'pilot project school'. Did 'pilot' mean temporary? Did 'pilot' refer to an 'experiment' that would undergo a programme evaluation in order to apply results elsewhere? Or, did 'pilot' signal a symbolic place-holder – a kind of 'foot in the door' – for a more permanent school? Dei's policy reference for his re-proposal (*Towards a new beginning*; see Ontario Government/African Canadian Community Working Group, 1992) was very clear that 'Focused schools' would be permanent stand-alone schools within the public realm.

Our emphasis on 'pilot' may appear innocuous at first, but Akande's general point about curriculum integration versus curriculum separation would figure prominently in relation to the development of the Africentric Alternative School. In fact, when the board was deliberating whether to approve the opening of the Africentric Alternative School, Wallace (2009: n.p.) noted that:

> [b]efore the Trustees' vote in January 2008, the media, which has played a significant part in perpetuating the segregation myth, also weighed in as all three major Toronto … [daily newspapers] condemned the proposal. The *Toronto Star* argued the 'idea smacks of segregation, which is contrary to the values of the school system and Canadian society as a whole,' while the *Globe* and *Mail* ran a column that called Black-focused schools 'as insulting as they are ridiculous.' Even more vehement in its criticism, the National Post said the 'concept of special schools for Black students is one of those terrible ideas that refuses to die'.

For some opponents, both Black and non-Black, Black-focused schooling represented a reprise of formal, racialised schooling in North America, the histories and geographies of slavery in Canada and the United States, and the doctrine of 'separate but equal' in the United States. Akande's questions about integration or separation also echoes the classic debates between W.E.B. Du Bois and Booker T. Washington roughly a hundred years earlier in the United States.

Later that year, Lloyd McKell, the new executive officer of Student and Community Equity for the TDSB, would lend his support for a Black-focused school to serve as a pilot project. McKell believed that 'a Black-focused pilot school for students who [were] too alienated to remain in the system would be helpful, offering more Black teachers, an Afro-centric curriculum and a more nurturing environment' (Brown, 2005b). However, McKell was careful to qualify his endorsement of a pilot school, and reinforced his lack of support for a separate system of schools for Black students, as he preferred to maintain the comprehensive ideal of public schools for students of all backgrounds (Brown, 2005b).

The news about McKell's, albeit heavily qualified, public support for the idea of a pilot Black-focused school in Toronto had immediate repercussions, particularly at the provincial level. For instance, the Conservative Premier Dalton McGuinty spoke out against the idea, arguing he had not seen any sound evidence that clearly demonstrated 'beyond a shadow of a doubt' that Black-focused schools would constitute an improved learning environment (Brennan and Brown, 2005). For McGuinty, students should be educated in an inclusive environment that met the needs of a broad range of children. In his own words, and seemingly overlooking the already segregated characteristics of Toronto and Toronto schools, he was 'much more comfortable with the concept of bringing children from a variety of backgrounds together and simulating the communities in which they [were] living and [were] going to have to grow up' (Brennan and Brown, 2005).

An entrepreneurial event

At this point in the development of the Africentric Alternative School, the idea of a Black-focused school in Toronto had (1) policy precedents; (2) moral arguments for and against establishment; (3) the involvement of policy actors, activists, entrepreneurs and subjects; and (4) rapidly emerging and divergent political fronts. Dei's idea of a pilot Black-focused school was connected to earlier policy recommendations of Toronto and Ontario. As noted in Chapter Two, in 1991 the New Democratic Party provincial government initiated a Black Secretariat. In 1992, a multilevel Ontario government working group (the Four-level Government/African Canadian Community Working Group) proposed ideas about Black-focused schooling. Their recommendations are contained in the report *Towards a new beginning*. The working group proposed targeted programmes called 'Focused School' in schools that had high percentages of Black students in each Toronto borough.

The moral arguments for Black-focused schools centred on a Black-oriented curriculum as a necessary intervention into persistent educational and social disadvantage for Black students. This meant arguing for curriculum change in existing public schools in addition to proposing separate 'Black-focused' schools. Before these programmes could be implemented, the new Conservative government disbanded the Black Secretariat in 1997. At this point, and given the emergence of the new TDSB in 1998, the idea of Black-focused schooling disappeared from public discourse. It was not until 2003 and 2004 that Angela Wilson, assuming a role of policy activist, used the dormant 'alternative schools' policy to advocate for Black-focused schooling.

The development of a Black-focused school began to shift from policy imaginations towards policy development. As such, imagination and moral pressure were necessary but insufficient conditions to develop the school. The policy development of creating a Black-focused school would be within the prevailing ideas of choice, and an alternative schools policy framework with an affinity with notions of parental choice in schooling. The development of the proposal invited a range of political outrage, as we have noted. It seemed that the only viable lever to develop a Black-focused school was to use a combination of the alternative policy and choice mechanisms. That is, the only viable lever was neoliberal policy after a decade of advocacy trying to ameliorate, and being constantly rebuffed from doing so, Black students' underachievement and marginalisation.

These kinds of tangled educational politics between political movements and seemingly contradistinctive individuated policy realms are what Pedroni (2007) described as 'tactical and opportunistic alliances' within education markets to secure educational opportunities. Markets provide opportunities and risks for enunciating racialised positions within the public educational sphere in ways that the juridical and the moral fields do not. As Rizvi and Lingard (2010: 9) noted, 'a commitment to market values in education does not entirely involve a rejection of a concern for social equity, but it does suggest that the meaning of equity is re-articulated'. In the event of the Africentric Alternative School, educational equity was pursued through tactical alliances which radically altered previous notions of equity on the basis of inclusion, and which reconfigured notions of equity on the basis of separation.

On 8 February 2005, just a few days after the St Lawrence Centre forum 'Making the grade: Are we failing our Black youth?', Wilson and Harrow met with TDSB assistant director Gerry Connelly and area superintendent Trevor Ludski to present their ideas for an Alternative Africentric School (*Toronto Star*, 18 November 2007). Later, Wilson and Harrow would meet with fellow advocates Beunah Livingstone and Suad Aimad to draft an alternative school proposal (*Toronto Star*, 18 November 2007). It was reported that it was unclear whether the proposal being drafted was for the purposes of a pilot school or pilot curriculum programme or a full-fledged alternative school. Nevertheless, the proposal would take a year to complete (*Toronto Star*, 18 November 2007).

As noted, Wilson and Harrow learned about the long dormant alternative school programme – that so many had used in the past – and were shrewd enough to use it to provide a policy opportunity for the school. Or, as Thompson and Wallner (2011: 818, our emphasis) put it: 'the proposal was politically viable due in part to the efforts of *policy entrepreneurs* and *more administratively viable* as compared to other policy alternatives'. Policies created previous to the pre-eminence of 'choice' in public schooling, such as the alternative schools programme, became located within a school-choice framework and, as such, racial politics were simultaneously circumscribed within this realm (Goldberg, 2009).

Racism without race: marketing a racialised brand

Just weeks after Lloyd McKell endorsed the idea of a Black-focused school, the TDSB initiated a series of programmes aimed to assess the viability of such an idea. In a regular meeting held on 21 September 2005 the TDSB received a written brief from the Programs and School Services Committee (PSSC), which had a subcommittee called the 'Africentric Advisory Committee'. During a special meeting on 29 August 2005, the committee provided updates and reported on: (1) a literature review and analysis entitled *African-centered schools in Toronto: Foundations and principles*; (2) the establishment of the Africentric Summer Institute for the summer of 2005 that was 'offered to 80 students in Grades 1 to 5 who are working at Level 2 or below in English and/or mathematics'; (3) the development of an Inclusive Curriculum Writing Project with an Africentric focus; and (4) the aim to 'initiate and facilitate the Process and Procedures for the establishment of an Africentric Alternative School' and to establish outreach communications to assess the support for a potential 'Africentric Alternative School' in the community (TDSB, 2005a: 880–1).

While each of these planned initiatives was instrumental in the eventual development of the Africentric Alternative School, the significance of the 29 August meeting rests with the removal of the term 'Black-focused schools', which was replaced in school board documents by the term 'Africentric Alternative'. At this point, the term 'Black-focused' was no longer used in board documents. An undated web document from the board explained the word selection: 'Within the Black community, there are people from a diversity of histories, cultures, customs, values and opinions. The term Africentric does not focus on race and instead, reflects the diversity of the community' (TDSB, nd: 1).

The introduction of the term 'Africentric' attempted to elide a racial focus in favour of one centred on ethnicity. The new name no longer evoked a school for racialised Blacks, and therefore attempted to avoid the segregationist accusations that accompany the invocation of race within the colour-blind discourses of Canadian multiculturalism. The new term, apparently, was the result of an estimation that a greater emphasis on ethnicity, rather than race, would provide the new school better traction with prospective parents and students. The name change would, hopefully, appeal to those who espoused Canada's colour-blind multicultural policies, or at least mitigate the strong negative reactions to the school that were aimed at the idea of using race as an identifier within colour-blind multicultural policies.

The name change appeared to be, therefore, a marketing attempt, though not a terribly successful one. Unfortunately, the term 'Africentric' did not 'test' well with 'focus groups' who self-identified as Black *and* Caribbean. The name change introduced a virulent politics of recognition that concerned the efforts to control and operationalise race (that is, 'Blackness') but which produced a contest between representations of Black that included the 'continent' (Africa) and the 'islands' (Caribbean). One board trustee remarked:

> 'There was definitely a very strong stream within Black communities [articulating a] 'Back to Africa', or 'Black-consciousness' school of thought – cause, god knows, Africans have a whole different concept of what 'Africentric' means. For instance, Caribbean parents were actually not interested in the Africentric school at all. Most African nationals, they're like, 'what are you talking about?' To me the point was we have to deal with the alienation that is present, rampant in Canadian Black communities in

Toronto and this concept [Africentric] exacerbated the problem.'

We discuss the issues of recognition and representation in more detail in Chapters Four and Five. What is important in this chapter is to note the concerted effort to brand a racialised product within existing educational markets, and ironically, to do so without reference to race.

The new brand of 'alternative' also functioned in unexpected ways. While the previous board's policy discourses that addressed at-risk Black students conveyed notions of justice and inequities within the school system, the recent name change in board policies broke the connection with the anti-racist rhetoric of the early 1990s and reformulated the discourse towards the principles of economic choice.

The (apparent) erasure of race, and the assertion of ethnicity, better enabled the idea of a Black-focused school within the existing choice framework. The erasure of race simultaneously positioned a potential school to compete with the roughly 30 other alternative schools (at the time, now in excess of 40), and the broader Toronto educational marketplace that included other educational brands, such as Catholic, Indigenous and Francophone schools.

The proposed Africentric Alternative School was *not* treated in the same way as other proposed alternative schools that were established at the same time as the Africentric school. These included: the Da Vinci Alternative School, a school based on Waldorf and Steiner education; the Grove Community School, with a social justice and environmental focus; and the Equinox Alternative School, with a holistic learning and teaching approach. All of these new schools were located within the bounds of the old Toronto board, with the Africentric Alternative School being the only alternative school located outside of the boundaries of the old board.

It was only with the Africentric school that there was extensive racialised contestation over who has the right to define the parameters of the market, that is, what alternative schools are acceptable – and debates over who controls culture. A brand became the precondition for the Africentric Alternative School to differentiate itself from other schools and the means for it to compete over student market share.

Neoliberalism as the 'solution' to debates over integration and separation

For the next 18 months, throughout 2006 and into 2007, a variety of Africentric programmes and curricula would be piloted in and around schools in the TDSB. It appears that most of these pilot programmes were intended to function as initial steps in a programme designed to integrate Black teachers, culture, epistemologies and heritages into the broader curriculum. During this time, a variety of important stakeholders would engage each other and form political blocs around the establishment of a Black-focused school. Most notable would be the Coalition of the African Canadian Organization (CACO).

While the CACO would officially endorse a separate Black-focused school, this was not unanimous, with a few coalition members unhappy with a political approach that looked to separate Black students from other students. Nevertheless, the prevailing CACO position would also rest upon the discourse of educational choice. For instance, Margaret Parsons, the executive director of the African Canadian Legal Clinic, a coalition partner, would remark that: 'For [White people school choice is] all about creating a level playing field. But when it comes to Blacks, it's segregation' (Chung, 2005). Furthermore, Parsons criticised Canada's policy of multiculturalism. In her view, multicultural policies blinded authorities to systemic racism against Blacks, even as they implemented inclusion and integration policies. 'It [multiculturalism] has done a disservice to us. It doesn't allow us to focus on communities that are in crisis and need a targeted approach. It does not address racism' (Chung, 2005).

Finally, the organisation Black Youth Taking Action (BYTA) held a rally at Ryerson University in May 2007 demanding the creation of a Black-focused school. The rally was designed to petition the decision to bar Malik Zulu Shabazz, the chair of the New Black Panther Party from entering Canada. At the subsequent press conference, Nkem Anizor, head of BYTA, advocated for a Black-focused school while stating:

> this generation of black youth, we went to school. We are not like our parents. We don't want your approval. We don't want to get tapped on the head. We don't want to move to the suburbs and be comfortable. What we want is freedom, justice and equality and we're going to use our education to get it. (*Toronto Star*, 16 May 2007)

As we have indicated, a major tension between ideas of integration and separation would emerge around the development of the Africentric Alternative School. This tension would produce feelings of betrayal from at least one board trustee who believed that the board pilot projects were designed towards the political strategy of integration, and not directed towards evaluation studies for the eventual development of a separate school (Interview with authors). On 12 June 2007, Wilson and Harrow met with board assistant director Gerry Connelly. The next day, their proposal was presented to the board's PSSC. The proposal was accepted, in principle, and sent to the board.

Fifteen days later, on 27 June 2007, the TDSB ratified policy P062. P062 defined the idea of 'alternative schools', listed their responsibilities and operational procedures (in PR.584), and provided guidelines for the creation and administration of such schools. Of course, over 30 alternative schools were already up and running, produced in one of the now defunct educational boards that had been amalgamated into the current TDSB. P062 defined an alternative school as one that practises an unique pedagogic approach, caters not only to particular needs but also to differentiated learning styles and preferences, and one that is separated from mainstream schools (although they may be housed within mainstream schools).

P062 highlighted the board's appreciation of the contributions of students, parents and staff to the success of alternative schools, and its commitment to foster such involvement and, more importantly, defined those schools as programme choices. The policy reiterated that: 'The Board is committed to developing and promoting alternative schools as viable pathway and program choices' (TDSB, 2007b: 1).

On the very day that P062 was ratified, the board requested staff to prepare a report on the feasibility of a 'pilot' Africentric Alternative School. Following this request, staff initiated consultations with community and staff stakeholders under the terms of the board's *Alternative schools policy and procedures*. Framed under this policy, the Africentric Alternative School became depicted as a choice option within the public system, seeking to meet the 'unique needs' of African Canadian children in Toronto. Six months of consultations would take place. On 29 January 2008, the trustees voted in favour of the Africentric Alternative School (11 to 9).

Postscript

This chapter did not explicate the epistemological influences or knowledge claims influencing the event of the school's becoming. Rather, this chapter explicated more of the ontological aspects affecting the policy event. The spatial and temporal analysis of this chapter illustrated how objects and subjects easily interchange positions depending on the location of the analysis.

For instance, the contingencies within the objects of race are now capitalised and normalised within education markets that operate around ideas of choice, selectivity and identity. This is why the actions of the two community activists Angela Wilson and Donna Harrow are so interesting, in using what was a dormant policy option to establish alternative schools. The determination to use any mechanism available, including school choice, sits within 'a politics of no longer waiting'. However, while the market demarcates and separates, it also limits. Support for the school, then, could be arguably devoid of race and based on providing choice. In fact, as one board trustee explained: 'So I was one of the councillors that supported it … So why did I support it? I believed that school choice is an important value for parents, having different options' (Interview).

The idea of choice, rather than any form of anti-racist politics, conjoined conservative and liberal politicians. The outcome of the Africentric Alternative School was already part of a complicated education politics, which in this instance, we suggest, is part of the contingency and continuity of the events of (privatised) race and choice schooling, buttressed and supported by educational neoliberalism in Toronto.

Neoliberalism and the commodification of identity

*There is an extensive literature, over the course of 25 years, that identifies neoliberalism as a political-economic theory that utilises the efficiencies of market economics to develop and legitimate government priorities and practices. Neoliberalism also promotes forms of social organisation that emphasise individuals' freedom of choice, and has emphasised ways to increase the educational choices of those who have been racialised as Black or African American. Neoliberalism calls for 'freedom', mostly understood in relation to the rights of the individual to market participation and of markets themselves to operate without interference from the state (Friedman, 1962, 1980).

Neoliberalism seeks to reduce the social, political and economic risks assumed by liberal (that is, democratic) governments, and instead transfer these risks onto individuals through their relationships with each other and, importantly, themselves. Neoliberalism provides mechanisms for self-regulation (that is, incentives, penalties) which involves the devolution of risk onto individuals who, in turn, become responsible for their own care (that is, they are 'empowered' to discipline themselves; Rose, 1999a). Neoliberal governmental practices are an entrepreneurial model via the fabrication of techniques that emphasise 'the greater individualization of society and the "responsibilization" of individuals and families' (Peters, 2001: 85).

Neoliberal education policy

Neoliberal education policy enunciates values that emphasise deregulation, consumer choice and competition. Consequently, neoliberal restructuring in education policy often involves shifts from central administration to managerial decentralisation coupled with new forms of public provision (for example, magnet and charter schools) and financing (for example, voucher programmes).

School-choice alternatives are grounded on (at least) three arguments: (1) with wider school choices the ability to exit underperforming public schools is distributed more fairly and socioeconomically disadvantaged students gain access to better schools; (2) a decentralised school system is more responsive to the different needs of students than schools dependent on a central district administration (Chubb and Moe, 1988); and (3) school-choice initiatives create a competitive market environment which forces all schools to improve their academic standards to respond to the quality demands of their 'consumers' (Chubb and Moe, 1990).

Under neoliberalism, educational institutions are not only expected to behave like actors in a market, but are also transformed by consumers' needs that respond to and shape the schooling choices within an education system. School-choice policies, then, are coupled with management technologies that are designed to 'marketise' choice of schools, technologies which include increased exposure to competition, increased accountability measures, and the implementation of performance goals and quality assurance measures (Davies and Bansel, 2007).

The enterprising subject

As a mode of government, neoliberalism refers to the tactics, mechanisms and other technologies used to persuade populations to discipline themselves economically and/or enterprisingly. Hence, neoliberalism alters how people are governed and refers to a shift from overt forms of control or 'oppression', and toward more covert forms of control imbued with individuals' own desires and active participation in the development of an entrepreneurial self. As Edwards (2002: 357) stated:

> [g]overning, therefore, has less to do with a rational process of social reform and more to do with fashioning conduct based on certain cultural norms and values, wherein individuals are responsible for consuming and enterprise. Thus, subjectivities are themselves re-fashioned in eliciting a particular image of human beings as enterprising.

In policy arenas, the educational 'entrepreneur' entirely rewrites the previous figure of the increasingly inert and defunct educational 'activist' championing moral attitudes of equality. In particular, there are redefined norms and values associated with an economised idea of equity and social justice. Neoliberal investments in education highlight how a liberal politics of education, organisation and mobilisation has been replaced by neoliberal tactics and strategies of leverage, branding and market share. Now, neoliberal education policies that promote self-responsibility and freedom of choice produce school markets in which families are 'empowered' and/or 'responsible' for selecting particular 'educational investments' (Foucault, 2008: 229).

Education policy, furthermore, provides entrepreneurial opportunities to develop schools to support self-identified educational investments. We suggest this is similar to Fraser's (2009) proposition that forms of politics such as second-wave feminism are far more complicated, and possibly contradictory, under neoliberal conditions. Thus '[a]spirations that had a clear emancipatory thrust in the context of state-organised capitalism assumed a far more ambiguous meaning in the neo-liberal era' (Fraser, 2009: 108).

Racial neoliberalism

As feminisms have changed, Goldberg (2009) has noted that similarly neoliberalism changed the registers of race and altered how these registers are used and controlled. The insertion of the market as the organising principle of government shifted the formal and 'oppressive' technologies of race and biopower into covert technologies of non-state action. The primary means of this shift was through individuation and increasing the 'responsibilisation' for 'cultural deficiencies' attributed to people of colour.

The individual is now responsible for race and any ameliorations deemed necessary around its use. Neoliberalism thus equivocates on notions of 'freedom' and 'equality', and suggests that any instantiation of these concepts will be done through the enactment of private preference. The withdrawal and deregulation of the neoliberal state reorders and downloads raciologies onto individuals. However, the withdrawn and deregulated state does not eradicate racism. The neoliberal state claims that if there are no racialised policies, then by definition there cannot be institutional racism – there is only individualised responsibility and deficit. In effect, neoliberal education policy that supports choice, and can seamlessly incorporate legacy initiatives like the alternative school programme, reshapes, conflates and brands, and empowers, ethnicity in racialised school quasi-markets. Comaroff and Comaroff (2009: 15, original emphasis) noted the economic implications from such strategies:

> Mark this term: *empowerment*. In the post-colony it connotes privileged access to markets, money, and material enrichment. In the case of ethnic groups, it is frankly associated with finding something essentially their own and theirs alone, something of their essence, to sell. In other words, a brand.

The neoliberal state explicitly downloads the liberal legacy of biopolitics onto individuals through the skilful use of policy that induces subjects to use race in ways that allow them to become 'empowered', 'responsible' and 'enterprising' for their own wants and needs. Race, then, continues to be a key biopolitical technology in the management of populations, especially in the sorting of those who are threats and those who need to be defended, both within and outside the neoliberalised state (Foucault, 2003). However, race operates within a context of inseparable connections to markets and to the effects of marketisation and commodification.

Private and public registers of racism

Goldberg (2009) argued that government's neoliberal devolution of risk produces new and different registers of raciology; registers through which race is invisibilised, erased and denied in the realm of the neoliberalised state policy terrains. For instance, multicultural policies that emphasise ethnicity rather than race are clear examples of how the state empowers its citizenry. Nevertheless, these neoliberal raciologies hardly indicate an absence of race and racism. Rather, the reduced, withdrawn, and deregulated state has reconfigured race but 'it has hardly disappeared. The State has been placed behind a wall of private preference expression, of privatized choice' (Goldberg, 2009: 334).

Private preferences (appear to) exonerate the state from explicit racism; however, our interest in neoliberal race and raciologies is in the manner with which these signifiers interact with markets, and how people use these signifiers within notions of freedom as articulated in logics of the market rather than, say, democracy. Thus, school-choice policies enunciate ideas of choice, freedom and equality, and invite policy entrepreneurs to develop schools for specific racialised positions. In the case of the Africentric Alternative School, neoliberal education policy that supports choice, and can seamlessly incorporate legacy initiatives like the alternative school programme, reshapes, conflates and brands ethnicity in racialised school quasi-markets. The use of school-choice policies is a way of using one's entrepreneurial freedom, of making one's educational investment, of enacting one's self-responsibility and of taking care of one's existence. School-choice policy is a way to survive racially.

The voluntary formation of human capital is a seductive means to govern when educational choice of differentiated curricula induces consumerist behaviour under the guise of empowerment and responsibilisation. The seduction is realised when the voluntary formation of human capital uses the racial categories provided by the Enlightenment.

Educational investments provided by the Enlightenment are now separated through private preference and school choice, and able to be pursued apart from the various oppressions encountered in the normal or common school (that is, racism, sexism, homophobia). The voluntary formation of human capital maintains schooling's connection to capitalism, and specifically labour production, but in ways that simultaneously legitimate racial groupings through voluntary separations.

In a rearticulation of equality, neoliberal education policy develops differentiated markets for entrepreneurial and innovative subjects that form human capital voluntarily and in ways that are both commensurate with and responsible for the Enlightenment category of race. Neoliberal government extends its Enlightenment project through a biopolitics of educational empowerment and responsibilisation, conveniently fulfilling the self-prophecies of 'agency', 'cause' or 'intention'.

Reflections

Attempting to redress anti-Black racism through neoliberalism is seemingly an odd choice. The peculiarity stems from an alternative conception about how the contemporary subject is composed, and how it acts within shifting economic and political landscapes. Traditionally, the raced subject (that is, the non-White subject) would be explained through a set of intrinsic traits or qualities (that is, biology) that impel the subject via a set of internal precepts and decisions (that is, epistemology) and moral codes (that is, culture) that shape resistance to the dominant White presence.

The racialised subject is an a priori subject that remains intact and immune to the influential effects of different environments. Our choice to use neoliberalism to explain the becoming of the Africentric Alternative School revives historical debates in the literature concerning how subjects are composed and represented, and how subjects act. We are keenly aware that this selection may perpetuate enactments of Whites discussing 'agency' in ways that circumscribe the actions of racialised others. With this caveat in mind, our goal, however, is to illustrate how these academic disputations neglect the policy environments that shape action and, specifically, neglect neoliberalism.

Our selection of neoliberalism is also problematic in that neoliberalism is often code for White researchers to explain White behaviour. This is often seen in school-choice studies. Rarely is neoliberalism used to explain the actions of subjects who have been racialised, even though a literature exists (Rofes and Stulberg, 2004), and a specific literature and debate for those racialised as Black or African American (Slaughter-Defoe et al, 2012). This is largely due to the explanation discussed in the preceding paragraph, but partly due to how neoliberalism is understood as both a political *and* economic form of governance.

More specifically, neoliberalism is largely absent in studies of race and racism because neoliberalism is often misunderstood as either a political *or* economic form of governance, not both.

If neoliberalism is used in conjunction with raced subjects, it is almost entirely used in either political or economic analyses in order to illustrate how racism is cloaked within 'post-racial' and 'colour-blind' discourses that reify racist practices while appearing progressive or benevolent. Neoliberal analyses that are constructed around 'post-racial' ideas then fit nicely within, and conveniently perpetuate, 'critical' paradigms that attempt to reveal hidden and suppressed contradictions. Our goal, however, is to illustrate how ideas of 'race', 'social justice' and 'schooling' have been constructed, altered and perpetuated in attempts to redress anti-Black racism rather than identify contradictions. That is, our critical approach is to problematise the very objects in play during the becoming of the school.

The reinscription of Whiteness

Afrocentric schooling and curricula have been rejected as being exclusive rather than inclusive – a rejection premised on an accusation that Afrocentric schooling uses a flawed notion of a unitary Black identity (Lund, 1998). However, the primary opposition to the establishment of Africentric schools similarly mobilises notions of separation, framing the school as a move to segregate the public school system.

The spectre of separation, when enunciated as part of opposition to the school, then occludes the ways in which low student achievement or historical exclusion have been and are endemic within public schooling. In effect, summoning the spectre of separation is a tactical means to reinscribe Whiteness within public schools. Afrocentric schools in Toronto are part and parcel of neoliberal policy of *not only* choice but *also* of consciously selecting a form of separation that allows one category to become marked as 'other', perhaps conveniently.

In the framework of colour-blind multiculturalism, Black-focused schools could be opposed by declaring them 'un-Canadian'. That is, Black-focused schools can be opposed because they contravene the assertion that race is absent in Canada and undermine the multicultural settlement. As we noted earlier, the assertion that race is absent denies a history of Black slaves in Canada and the demolishing of identifiably Black urban areas such as Africville in Nova Scotia in the 1960s (Nelson, 2008). The opposition to Black-focused schools converts the assertion of political power and the need to address systemic historical disadvantage into a threat to national identity, and they are, of course, threats to particular fables that perpetuate that identity.

In this political environment, the Africentric Alternative School is constituted as separate in ways that other forms of 'alternative' schools are not. Ironically, opposition to Africentric schooling based on issues of segregation and separation simply denotes the continued salience of race and racism in Canada. This particular use of choice policy means that qualifiers are used to justify the elision of race and racism, and a White version of national belonging in Canada.

The fragility of racial schools

Neoliberal education policy is most seductive in political formations that are fragile and constantly being re-territorialised through personal choices that are legitimated in markets. Neoliberal education policy highlights that choice is normalised and ubiquitous, and therefore opposition to the Africentric Alternative School cannot, and did not, radically curtail the development of it – for this would mean challenging *all* schools opened under market policies. The key is that it matters *who* is using market opportunities and for what *purposes*; for example, 'segregation' was coded within support and opposition to education policies and schools.

Identity itself is thus marketised, in that opposition to choice is based on particular mobilisations of legitimacy in the market. Africentric schools, even when operating as sites of solidarity and necessity in response to ongoing disadvantage or location in a racialised geopolitical context, are unlike Christian schools or language schools (e.g. French Immersion).

This rearticulation of educational equity also highlights identity as a fragile terrain for neoliberal education politics (Youdell, 2011). The policy landscape pertaining to the establishment of the Africentric Alternative School enunciates a reconfigured concept of equity within the fragility of identity. It leaves the school constantly vulnerable and susceptible to ongoing racialisation and racism. It points to the necessary and continual engagement with the question of what is a legitimate manifestation in an education market – what counts as a 'legitimate' school and to what extent does neoliberal schooling contribute to emancipatory efforts, if at all?

Choice schools are still regulated in the ways discussed above, and in ways that operate through a performativist culture of the self 'to what might be regarded as a regime that involves observation, surveillance, and examination in the form of monitoring of learning, intervention, "programmes", and assessments' (Foucault, 1982: 50). Neoliberal education policy maintains schooling as the disciplinary and reproductive machine that it always has been. But now neoliberal schooling is the disciplinary and reproductive machine of self-selected investments.

In the end, the contradictions of neoliberal education equality remain deeply indebted to Enlightenment constructions of the self and to the disciplining practices of schools. In this sense, however, the voluntary formation of human capital is a statement about how education discipline is now distributed more equally.

The weight of racialised schools

Segregation was used to locate the debate about Afrocentric schooling in a particular dichotomy (inside/outside) that invoked 'the weight of race', to use Goldberg's (2009: 9) formulation. This is:

> [t]hat weight borne ... differentially, borne by some for others ... The weight of race lingering between the scales of justice bound by a past, present and future, distributed and redistributed between those marked indelibly by history and those seeking incurably to make themselves outside of history's cast ...

This is weightlessness as colour-blindness in the nation. The continued saliency of the nation as place, in which decisions can be made about who gets to belong or not belong – what Hage (1998) called the role of 'spatial managers' – is evident in much of the opposition to the Africentric Alternative School.

The disproportionate weight of race alters how equality is sought through neoliberal education policy based on separation by choice. Separation by choice acknowledges the stark racial separations that have operated covertly and disproportionately for particular groups. Thus, a politics of self-separation provides a register to articulate inequalities that have not been dealt with sufficiently. Within this politics of self-separation, the entrepreneurial subject produced through neoliberalism is 'freer' to leave the racisms of liberalism.

More importantly, school-choice policies provide mechanisms to address historic inequalities, at least in the sense of separating oneself from these histories. School-choice policies certainly will not redress racisms; however, school-choice policy does provide entrepreneurs and other enterprising subjects with opportunities to speak for themselves and to take responsibility for themselves against persistent and historical educational inequalities. The price for this equality, however, is separation.

How one cares for and maintains the separations that provide entrepreneurial opportunities is paramount. The aporia of education policy equality is no longer invested in debates between democratic and capitalist ideologies – these ideologies have been merged. In its (re)creation, the self constantly positions itself within market niches and racial brandings that provide its very articulation. The self must care for racial separations because neoliberal educational equality depends on market separations.

FOUR

'Up in the northwest corner of the city': the city, race and locating the school

Once the Toronto District School Board (TDSB) supported the establishment of an Africentric Alternative School, the event of becoming-school added an additional layer of spatial or locational politics. Like the years preceding the deciding vote at the TDSB, the question of where the school would be located would be become part of the race politics of the city.

The politics involved in the selection of a suitable location for the school would naturally appear to be the culminating event, following the political and entrepreneurial activities identified in the preceding chapters. This chapter, therefore, appears to be chronologically, the obvious one to be a last chapter in research on policy 'implementation'. For instance, if the school was not approved by the board, then there would be no discussion about where to locate the school.

However, our argument is based upon the idea that the question of location affected the entire process of the becoming of the school rather than just at the 'end' of a sequential process. The question of location 'haunted' trustees and community members prior to any governance and policy-development activities designed to produce the school. The city of Toronto was powerfully shaped by various racial, spatial and economic factors that functioned as strong preconditions for the becoming of the school. In fact, the question about 'where to put the Black school in the White city' would produce strong feelings across Toronto, given its long and troubled histories with placements of non-White populations (and their placements in relation to each other). As such, we have decided to place this chapter in 'the middle' of the book in order to illustrate how the city powerfully influenced the becoming of the school.★

In this chapter we examine the event of finding a location for the school, and the connections between the ways in which the city was (and is) racialised and undergoing urban change around gentrification and 'rebranding' of neighbourhoods. We examine the connections between education policy, cities and the new forms of suburbia in multicultural cities.

The search for a home

On 2 April 2008, during a meeting of the Program and School Services Committee (PSSC), members of the Africentric School Support Committee (ASSC), including Donna Harrow, Emanuel Wanzama and Leslie Moody, presented an update on the Africentric Alternative School proposal. The ASSC presented for consideration the following recommendations for the operational model of the Africentric Alternative School:

a Preference for a junior kindergarten to grade twelve programme.

b Selection of a school facility, which was accessible by public transit and could provide opportunities for a varied academic program, extra-curricular activities and parent involvement facilities.

c Preference for locating the AAS [Africentric Alternative School] in a stand-alone (closed) site, on the grounds that such a site would afford greater flexibility in shaping the overall school environment consistent with the vision for the school. (*East York Mirror*, 2008)

After the update of the ASSC delegation, the PSSC agreed the next step was selecting the school site. Staff identified and reviewed 11 potential sites, including 3 non-operating sites, as possible locations. The following factors were considered by the committee: (a) utilisation rates which included use of classroom space; (b) projected enrolment trends; (c) Toronto Transit Commission public transport accessibility; (d) community demographic information; (e) condition of the facilities; and (f) related cost implications of possible facility upgrades. This committee also looked at whether the school should be a 'stand-alone' school or a 'school within a school', the latter form constituting how most alternative schools in Toronto were operated.

The six factors identified were primarily district budget considerations, and perhaps one that dealt with mobility issues within the city. While this was a feasible and considered approach to facilities planning, what the minutes of the committee omitted were the politics of race, culture and education in Toronto that would surround the selection of a location for the school. This spatial politics would provide evidence of how the school would quite quickly become an emerging, racialised object within a long and storied history of a racialised (and segregated) city. The politics of location would become explicit within the historical territories already mapped within the racialised city.

The primary suggestion for the location of the school was somewhere in the northwest of the city in an area that had a high proportion of Black residents and, it was assumed, potential Black students for the proposed school. These areas included wards of trustees who had voted for and against the school. Trustees who voted against the school pushed back against it being located in their wards. One trustee who voted for the school noted:

> 'Local councillors basically pushed back, I was surrounded by councillors that voted against it and if you're gonna vote against it the political will on the ground is not gonna see it happen. So they want it up in the northwest corner of the city where we have the highest concentrations of communities of African extraction. They wanted it up there but they had enormous problems with [trustees who voted against the school].' (Interview)

The refusal to have the school in certain wards was seen by some trustees to reinforce disadvantages for areas of the city that lacked services and infrastructure. One trustee who voted for the school, claimed that trustees who refused to have the school were in areas that had 'not only a majority of Black people but ... [also] where poverty exists on a huge scale' (Interview). By refusing to have a school in an area, these trustees were 'taking one more resource out of that neighbourhood' (Interview). As the decision continued to be deferred, trustees quickly conflated issues of race and class when discussing where to locate the school. Rather than identify the school as a beacon of anti-racist politics, the prevailing economic discourse – such as resourcing, space, and so forth – became the only way, or so it appeared, to constitute issues of racial equality.

The school within a school within a city

Lloyd McKell, TDSB's executive officer of student and community equity, explained that the decision to make the Africentric Alternative School a school within a school was a 'made-in-Toronto solution'. It would provide opportunities for staff collaboration 'because in actual fact, we want it to be a place where we can develop some of the best practices (for engaging black students) so we can share them with all schools [...] It has to be a unique environment with its own unique approach, but there's no point in having a school where we learn things other teachers cannot share' (Brown, 2008a).

Importantly, McKell introduced additional factors, such as professional development and teacher collaboration, albeit implicitly, into discussions about where the school ought to be located. With his comments, McKell altered the prevailing discourse of anti-poverty that some trustees mentioned, and reconfigured the reasonable, but insufficient, factors that focused on the budget considerations of the district. With this move, McKell subtly infused the proposed school with the exemplary and model status of unique pedagogical practices, and identified it as a conduit of district learning about Africentric knowledge.

Furthermore, McKell argued, Sheppard Public School was chosen from among 11 possible sites, partly due to public transit accessibility and facilities (for example, two gyms and a large playground). Moreover, the site had available space to contain an elementary alternative school due to declining enrolments. Additionally, it was argued that the preferred location was, as noted, in ward where a trustee had voted in favour of the school.

Over the years, Sheppard had experienced a significant drop in enrolments, causing claims of an inefficient use of resources, such as unused classrooms, and forcing the school board to lay off teachers. The trustee for the ward in which the school would be located, James Pasternak, claimed it would help Sheppard Public School with declining enrolment and incorporate a special programme that would not be totally separate from the regular school system. Moreover, he claimed, 'because it's a school within a school it's very fiscally responsible' (Interview) and argued its ward had enough community partners and resources to support the operation of the school. Sheppard was already running two after-school Black heritage programmes when it was proposed as the site of the Africentric Alternative School (Brown, 2008a). The politics of locating the school became buttressed with ideas of 'concentration' of Black-focused education.

Alternatively, a trustee who voted against the school disputed these reasons:

> 'Well, number one they've put it to a school that is not self-contained because they share with Sheppard. [The] school shares the two schools simply because other people within the community, other parents, did not want the kids at a sole Africentric school. So what would have been the

best thing to do if the board was strategic in their thinking, would be to look for a school that was actually a closed school that was in the proper locale, it didn't matter the ward, but look for closed school and have a specific point of bussing, transportation from the parents at certain locales to drop the kids off, pick them up at this time, for that school.' (Interview)

Conversely, a trustee who voted for the school considered that Pasternak had been very clever in taking the school into his ward, as that the ward, like other parts of the northwest, had the:

'same community, same issues you know, same levels of poverty, all that kind of stuff. And James [Pasternak] was really smart because taking this school and putting it within a larger school allowed him to save his school. Because the Sheppard Street School had this tiny little population and half the school wasn't being used. And we were just starting the process of closing schools and consolidating and all that kind of stuff, so politically it was really smart for him, to say nothing of the fact that he, you know, he really took it on the chin I think.' (Interview)

The Sheppard principal, Ira Applebaum believed that Sheppard would benefit from having more students, and its diverse student population made it a good fit for a culturally focused programme like the Africentric Alternative School: 'We have 35 languages spoken in our school and by bringing in teachers and a focus on Africentric programs, we'll infuse everyone's cultural perspectives' (Brown, 2008a). Regarding the curriculum to be taught by the new Africentric school, McKell clarified it would not just be an extended version of Black History Month:

We're not just teaching the achievements of people of African descent [...] We want teachers to incorporate a mix of cultural perspectives that are truly inclusive, that address the experiences of children of all backgrounds, including people of African–Canadian descent [...] And then we can learn from each other. (Brown, 2008a)

In referencing enrolments for the new school and potential space, McKell argued that if interest in the programme proved to be strong, then there were enough classrooms on two floors to accommodate more than one class per grade. However, if enrolments were low in the higher grades the programme could start in the lower grades first and the 'grow the enrolment' year by year, even as high as grade eight, if demand justified it (Brown, 2008a).

On 21 April 2008 the ASSC met with the Sheppard Public School council to share information with about the proposed Africentric school. On 25 April, Ira Applebaum sent a letter to Sheppard Public School parents describing the AAS pilot programme as an 'exciting opportunity' and saying it would be open to children of any background across Toronto, from junior kindergarten to grade five, who would wish to enrol in September 2009 (Brown, 2008a).

The Program Area Review Team (PART) held a meeting on 1 May 2008 with parents, teacher representatives and the principal of Sheppard Public School, alongside local community members, school council representatives and principals of the schools in the area, two representatives of the ASSC, the superintendent of education NW2, Trustee James Pasternak for Ward 5, and central staff of the board. Maria Augimeri – the city councillor for Ward 5 and a former school trustee in the area – attended the meeting and spoke in favour of locating the Africentric school at Sheppard Public School as an attempt to address the lack of pride among some Black students that could lead to dropouts, crime and violence. 'Will it be the answer to [reducing the] dropout rate among so many kids of colour? Maybe not, but we have to try,' claimed Augimeri. 'But the dropout rate is only an outcome of the problem – the root cause is poverty, and we should feel ashamed to live in a city so rife with poverty and violence' (Brown, 2008c).

There were 60 people present at the meeting, 48 parents and community members, and 12 TDSB staff. The co-chair of the ASSC, community worker Donna Harrow, presented the vision for the Africentric Alternative School. She contended it was 'putting forward an alternative to students feeling alienated and unattached from (sic) education'. As she put it, dropout rates among Black students constituted an issue that they had 'to look straight in the eye and do something about', as there were too many youngsters who were failing.

Once her presentation was finished, she answered questions from the audience. There were nearly two hours of questions including: 'Would the school be just for struggling students? – No'; or 'Would there be free bussing from other parts of the city? – No'; or 'How much autonomy the board will give the programme. – The board has a policy of honouring the particular vision of each alternative school.' After the question period, parents and community members filled in a written questionnaire where the majority welcomed the AAS under the roof of Sheppard Public School, with 37 votes favour, 3 against, 6 not sure, and 2 abstaining (Brown, 2008b).

The school council then held a meeting in which it voted to endorse the location of the alternative school in an unused section of the Sheppard school site. 'Why not? I think it's a wonderful idea to help kids know their roots,' said Rachel Moore, the Guyana-born chair of the school council. In her view, the school might not work in boosting Black students' engagement, 'but at least we can say we tried. Anything that can encourage kids in any little way is worth trying' (Brown, 2008b).

Following the school council endorsement, the proposal went to a school board committee and to the full school board for approval on 7 May and 21 May 2008 respectively.

Final decision for location

On 7 May 2008 the PART presented a report to the PSSC proposing the programme and operational model for the Africentric Alternative School opening in September 2009. The report provided a recap on the formation of the ASSC and the efforts made to inform the community and promote enrolment. It also detailed the goals and key highlights of the Africentric programme, the starting grade configuration and enrolment, and described the resources, implementation and review processes. Based on the PART report, the PSSC recommended the following:

a   That Sheppard Public School be designated as the site for the Africentric Elementary Alternative School as a shared-use facility;

b   That the Africentric Alternative School be offered as a JK–Grade 5 program at the Sheppard Public School site with growth as follows to include Grades 6, 7 and 8: Grade 6 in September 2010; Grade 7 in September 2011; Grade 8 in September 2012;

c   That the opening of the Africentric Alternative School in September 2009 be subject to an appropriate minimum enrolment to permit at least one class in at least two consecutive single or combined grades, such enrolment to be determined through a formal registration process completed in the early spring of 2009;

d That a school administrator be appointed in January 2009 to supervise the process for establishing the program and curriculum elements, staffing, resourcing, and school start-up arrangements required for school opening;

e That an Africentric Alternative School Steering Committee of parents, community members, staff and other appropriate members be established to support the process of establishing the school in accordance with operational procedure PR.584: Alternative Schools. (TDSB, 2008)

TDSB voted on 21 May 2008 to approve the recommendations, with a vote of 13 to 8. An Africentric school had found a home in Toronto.

The racialised northwest of the city

While the Africentric school had found a home, it had also been part of the ways in which race shapes, and is shaped, by the city. The location of the school in Sheppard Public School near the intersection of Keele Street and Sheppard Avenue West, is an area of the city variously known as University Heights, or Northwood Park, and bounding part of the city known vernacularly as Jane and Finch. The northwest has been called 'in-between cities' or 'inner suburbs' (Boudreau et al, 2009); 'metropolitan areas considered to be neither part of the downtown or centre city nor part of the suburban countryside' (Dippo and James, 2011: 116). These areas in Toronto are deemed to be:

> 'troubled' neighbourhoods within the city boundaries of Toronto ... [that] appear to be cultureless wastelands – no important political or business decisions happen here, and there are no important arts or entertainment venues, no important sporting events, no important culinary secrets. (Dippo and James, 2011: 123)

The northwest includes neighbourhoods that Hulchanski (2010) and colleagues identify as 'City #3' in their report on 'three cities within Toronto'. The Africentric school is in 'a generally low-income area of Toronto, in which neighbourhood incomes have fallen substantially over the past few decades compared to the ... [Toronto Census Metropolitan Area] average' (Hulchanski, 2010: 1). As one trustee noted:

> 'if you look at a map of Toronto I would argue the [school is in one of the] most geographically isolated neighbourhoods in Toronto because it's cut off by the 401 and it's cut off by all the big highways ... York University is on the, like this big cow pasture, right, like up there and then there's highways and then there's the rest of Toronto. So this is a community that is incredibly geographically isolated, that is bound together by poverty, by race, by all kinds of other things. It has no economic bases, there's no economy there other than the university and they're not hiring from the neighbourhood, you know what I mean, like that kind of stuff. There's Yorkdale Mall, you know what I mean ... there's just nothing.' (Interview)

Advocates for the school were careful to denote that the school was *not* in Jane and Finch. However, for one trustee who voted against the school, the idea that the school would not be located in Jane and Finch was counterbalanced by its role as a choice school, which could attract students from all over Toronto. As this trustee argued:

> 'Are people gonna come up from downtown Toronto and Scarborough or somewhere to bring the kids to Keele and Sheppard, which could be classified as Jane and Finch, that's a bad thing, I'm not sendin' my kid to Jane and Finch. And look where they put it you know?' (Interview)

(As an aside, after a couple of years of operation it turned out the majority of students enrolled in 2011/12 were from the northwest of Toronto, with fewer than 10 students from the more affluent southeast areas of the city [James et al, 2015].)

In a similar manner, Boudreau et al (2009) suggested that while Jane and Finch described the intersection of two arterial roads, Jane Street and Finch Avenue West, '"Jane and Finch" ... [was] an idea as much as it is a physical place' (2009: 122). The boundaries of Jane and Finch 'both as a physical place and as an idea ... [were] not easily pinned down' (2009: 122). While the Africentric school was adjacent to Black Creek Valley, the eastern boundary of Jane and Finch, the imaginary of the northwest was strong and closely connected to how race, ethnicity and the city were interconnected as types of place-brands.

Jane and Finch/York University Heights and rebranding

The inner suburban areas of Toronto are the new suburban context that does not manifest decay and poverty through dilapidated and abandoned buildings and vehicles. As Dippo and James outline:

> Rather, there are streets and streets of detached and semi-detached houses, bungalows and townhouses, shopping centres and strip malls, fast food and doughnut shops, parking lots and parkettes, and clusters of high-rise condominiums and apartment buildings. The ordinariness of these neighbourhoods often conceals the social problems related to poverty and hunger, the unemployment and underemployment, the street crime and violence that would mark them as 'inner city' suburbs. (Dippo and James, 2011: 118–19)

Like the rest of the city, which was undergoing gentrification, the northwest of the city was involved in various changes, from new business developments, including the area of University Heights, in which the Africentric school was to be located. It was an 'improving' area, according to the lists of ranked neighbourhoods put out by various Toronto magazines and websites, mostly because of new developments and services driven by York University. The area continued to be identified as distinct from Jane and Finch, which continued to be condemned as one of the worst places to live.

This reputation was the target of urban 'renewal' programmes two years before the school was located in Sheppard. The northwest was part of a 'rebranding', including Jane and Finch, for example, to incorporate University Heights – which is also known as Northwood Park. A press release from the ward councillor Anthony Perruzza stated that: 're-branding will bring the community and the university together, continuing to fight the neighbourhood's reputation for violence and hopelessness' (Nairin, 2012: 55). Nairin suggested that rebranding was a form of suburban gentrification of Jane and Finch connected to infrastructure, including transport, and new cultural and educational institutions. In October, 2008 the area around the intersection of Jane and Finch was festooned with purple banners declaring the area to be 'University Heights'. This rebranding garnered opposition from members of the Jane and Finch community.

Nonetheless, Concillour Perruzza declared that he did not understand the fuss:

> 'What would they like to name it?' Perruzza said from city hall. 'Jane and Finch is an intersection, it's not a name. It's not part of our signposts ... This intersection will continue to exist. Jane will continue to be a street. Finch will continue to be a street. The four corners will continue to be there.' Rather than a refutation of the neighbourhood's identity, said Perruzza, he likes to think of the University Heights rebrand as a 'gift box' ... And besides, said Perruzza, 'I'm not inventing anything new. The area was designated University Heights [by the city] and it has a number of other names. Those names have been forgotten, and I'm just dusting them off and letting them know that we have a history, and we will continue to build on that history in a positive way.' (Aveling, 2009)

Although the politics of place became a significant issue in the proposed rebranding, it was not a recent issue. While the councillor had hoped that names could just be 'dusted' off, Jane and Finch was an area of the city that was marked out as: 'a poorly planned, ugly, dangerous, and undesirable place in the city – a suburban ghetto. This branding ... [was] continually renewed over the last several decades by repeated representations of the district in the mass media as a troubled and dangerous area' (Interview). It was an area of the city that was not included when Toronto was put forward as an exemplar of the global, multicultural city.

Ethnicity and the city

In Toronto, the policy frames that linked business improvement with ethnicity also provided an indication as to the possibilities and limits of empowerment in relation to cultural identity. Toronto had a set of discourses that consider ethnicity as a marketable and essentialised form; however, this reduced the nuances and complexities of other discourses of ethnicity. Namely, some forms of ethnic difference were more palatable when connected to consumption.

When consumption is tied to education – such as choosing the Africentric Alternative School in an education market – identifiers such as Black and Africentric move onto more fraught terrain than a neighbourhood with 'authentic' cuisine or 'A Thousand Villages' ethnic free-trade wares. The Africentric Alternative School was a form of ethnicity that was both intelligible and unintelligible in the racialised geography of the city – the school was now to be a physical rather than phantasmic presence, it invoked the material threat of race, rather than benign difference and diversity (see Goldberg, 2009; Gulson, 2011). While the Africentric Alternative School could be established through policy, it was simultaneously set loose by the ostensive neutrality of choice policy (as discussed in Chapter Three) and so entered the registers of commodification and ethnicity that were racialised and (re)articulated in Toronto.

Toronto's geography and its history provided registers that recognised and identified different racial and ethnic identities. Prior to the Second World War, Toronto was primarily a WASP (White, Anglo-Saxon, Protestant) city. After the war, the migrant make-up changed, to the point that it is now the most ethnically and culturally diverse city in Canada (Buzzelli, 2001), as noted by some trustees: 'for all intents and purposes Toronto's a Black city'; 'we live in a more identity-conscious city than anyone else'.

The spatial politics of the Africentric Alternative School were rooted within this geo-history, in which the resistance to the school was constituted and constitutive of race and ethnic relations established within the city of Toronto. When asked to explain how the city of Toronto was racially stratified, a trustee noted that: 'ethnic communities tend to congregate [in Toronto] around religious institutions, churches, mosques, synagogues, community centres, shops, so you do have people of national extractions living in a community' (Interview).

It seemed inevitable that the politics of segregation regarding the Africentric Alternative School would be intertwined with the spatial politics of the city.

Summary

The establishment of the Africentric Alternative School can be understood, in part, by how it fitted onto Toronto's grid of race, ethnicity and class. Boudreau et al (2009: 98) proposed that:

> While both sides of this problematic of immigration and racialization meet in the reality of settlement and urban restructuring in Toronto, the economic prosperity of the metropolis evades many of the city's racialized

immigrant groups, as wealth and prosperity are increasingly concentrated amongst the white upper middle classes in the central core of the city and in certain suburbs. Diversity as a good-weather motto for a multi-ethnic metropolis is beginning to wear thin as a strategy for togetherness, in a city divided geographically and socio-economically along class and racialized lines.

Additionally, the racialised commodification of ethnicity occurred through the movements through the city. In other words, alternative-choice schools in TDSB were established to 'open boundaries' that destabilise the historical practices of catchment and provide consumers of race-based education with a market in which to participate. Through these movements, a market for choice schools was developed, and the commodification of race followed through the selection and consumption of the Africentric Alternative School. One trustee noted: 'I also messaged on school boundaries and the reality was ... if you wanna talk about so-called segregation you go look at these school boundaries, don't lecture my Afrocentric parents, let's start removing these school boundaries and make sure there's more integration' (Interview).

Here, the term 'integration' is used in relation to a city already marketised in relation to difference. As such, the spatial racial politics of Toronto were not created by searching for a location for the Africentric Alternative School; rather, the Africentric Alternative School was located on a highly contentious grid of racialisations already mapped onto the city.

Spatialising race within a moving city

Cities and education policy

*The ways that difference is produced and reconfigured through and due to race connects cities and education (Gulson, 2011; Lipman, 2011). Schools and policy are, furthermore, part of urban networks that 'are complex: they interact and interfere with each other in ways which are not predictable and which produce *emergent* forms of social organization in ways which cannot be foreseen' (Amin and Thrift, 2002: 129). These forms of social organisation are spatial, where space can be considered as emergent and exigent to social relations.

This is 'space' as 'relational space', dependent on multiplicity, on an overlapping rather than conterminous heterogeneity (Massey, 2005; Murdoch, 2006). Thrift (2003: 2022, cited by Nayak, 2010: 2378) suggested that '[s]paces can be stabilised in such a way that they act like political utterances, guiding subjects to particular conclusions'. Policy attempts to stabilise the uncertainty and unpredictability of space, and simultaneously the provisional permanence of space stabilises the incoherence and uncertainty of policy. Education policy is a technology that organises and arranges space and time, such as the opening and closing of schools and the reconfiguring of a separate school into a school within a school.

Education policy that establishes markets in education reorders urban space, such as the ways in which school choice encourages, though does not ensure, mobility, and encourages students to travel across a city to schools. Policy can, perhaps, be considered as part of 'networks of control' (Amin and Thrift, 2002: 128) that:

> snake their way through cities [and] are necessarily oligoptic, not panoptic: they do not fit together. They will produce various spaces and times, but they cannot fill out the whole space of the city – in part because they cannot reach everywhere, in part because they cannot know all spaces and times, and in part because many new spaces and times remain to be invented. (2002: 128)

This multiplicity also depends on the contingency of proximity and distance (Allen, 2003), where these are not only about measurement, for 'distance – like difference – is not an absolute, fixed and given, but is set in motion and made meaningful through cultural practices' (Gregory, 2004: 18). For example, on the one hand, a city becomes an aggregated area where a school, produced through school choice, is no longer located in a neighbourhood, but rather is part of the overall mobility of the city – dependent only on the forms of transport and access, and its viability in the neoliberal and consumerist imaginary, and its capabilities to change the reputation of a neighbourhood (for example, a neighbourhood where violence occurs, a neighbourhood with a 'good' school). On the other hand, a school cannot escape its neighbourhood, and the many ways in which places are established as areas of 'disadvantage' or areas to be 'feared'. These in/compossibles – mobility, buying power, various effects of fear and redemption – are assembled through the power of a city's geography.

Schools can be understood as places, but not static bounded entities, rather '[p]laces not as points or areas on maps, but as integrations of space and time, as spatio-temporal events' (Lorimer, 2008: 130). The idea of place as event is not a stable point, but is dependent on the coextensive nature of time and space which problematises the idea that place operates as a reference point – for example, the school is in 'that' area of the city. For, as Massey (2005: 139) asked: '[i]f there are no fixed points then where is here?' For, 'if "here" is the aggregation of multiple meetings and encounters that create a history, then what has come before is implicated in and constitutive of the multiple spatio-temporalities of now – that is now then and there' (Massey, 2005: 139).

Multicultural cities and suburbia

If spatial relations are 'open, provisional achievements', there is a need to examine how this relationality comes to be constituted. Anderson and Harrison (2010: 16) maintain, 'it becomes necessary to think through the specificity and performative efficacy of different relations and different relational configurations'. One example in the multicultural city is the development of new ideas of suburbia, such as the 'in-between city'. As Dippo and James (2011: 119) posited:

> suburbs today do not necessarily conform to the stereotype of homogeneity and affluence. Instead, suburbia is likely to be socially and culturally diverse, often with conditions that are much more like the 'inner city' in terms of social and political marginalization, economic exclusion, conflict with schools and the police, nutrition-related health issues, and a host of other effects of poverty and racism.

Canadian cities have been constituted in public media as versions of 'ethnoburbia' (DeWolf, 2004, cited by Dippo and James, 2011), and multiculturalism as a key part of suburbia has been raised in the literature on cities and difference in Australia (for example, Collins, 2000).

The location of difference in suburbia is in contrast to the historical constitution of the inner city as the realm of difference. Increasingly it is the 'inner suburbs' that new immigrants are calling home for their first port of call. Some new immigrant groups rent and have low incomes, and as such 'the option of remaining in the inner city will be seriously compromised as gentrification takes hold and access to affordable housing disappears' (Murdie and Teixeira, 2011: 20). The move of new immigrants to 'inner suburban neighbourhoods' and the reversal of historical settlement patterns creates 'a highly differentiated suburban ethnic geography' (Murdie and Teixeira, 2011: 20).

However, not only is there a differentiated, suburban, ethnic geography that is continually being recreated, there is also a city-wide process of differentiation acting upon different ethnic geographies evident in 'multicultural cities'. These geographies are premised on the continued contestation over what is permissible as culture in cities, and what are permissible visualisations of the multiculture (see Keith, 2005: 125 for a discussion of this). This contestation occurs concomitantly with the neoliberalising of cities and their various unfoldings of multiculturalism (for example, Hackworth, 2007), and is inexorably linked to – indeed, has a harmonious resonance with – the compulsory functions of schooling and its own pre-existent grid of racial and ethnic differentiation and categorisation, and its historical role in assimilating difference.

For Canadian cities like Toronto, particularly in the years following 1995, this has involved the creation of difference as a commodity, and hence 'makes ethnic diversity into a marketable commodity' (Boudreau et al, 2009: 20). This occurred alongside Toronto's governance being transformed into 'the entrepreneurial city, which resembles more of a business firm than a public institution' (Boudreau et al, 2009: 20), and the idea of 'the revanchist city, where more often than not the socially disadvantaged are also criminalized and where the middle classes have largely obliterated spaces of the poor through gentrification and social exclusion' (Boudreau et al, 2009: 20). School choice is an exemplary and harmonious mechanism of the entrepreneurial city in its efforts to reterritorialise places, either through fleeing undesirable school catchments or establishing new locales.

As such, within the neoliberal(ised) city, culture takes on an important role in the constitution of city space. This is particularly evident in what is termed the 'branding' of cities (and their schools), that is aimed at those who live outside of the city – and 'outside' often refers to a global network of cities rather than those within a national frame. As Hubbard noted: 'contemporary forms of place promotion are not simply attempts to advertise the city. Rather, the intention is to reinvent or rewrite the city, weaving myths which are designed to position the city within global flows of urban images and representational practices' (2006: 87).

This idea of weaving a myth is interesting, for it might also be applicable to what occurs internally in multicultural cities like Toronto. Furthermore, there may be no more mendacious myths than those produced from schooling about the possibilities of economic and social mobility that dovetail with the preferred images for global flows. That is, both the rebranding of 'troubled' areas through renaming so as to occlude a history of stigmatisation, and the identification of ethnicity with places for consumption produce a likely ersatz advertisement.

This identification of ethnicity with place endures long after the bodies of immigrant populations have left, such that, as Hackworth and Rekers noted: '[t]he values of multiculturalism are highly marketable in certain cases, so many ethnic commercial strips have remained, well after their resident community fled for the suburbs' (2005: 232). As multiple generations of migrants have left these parts of the city, as in other multicultural cities around the world such as Sydney and London, these names have remained as part of emerging 'cultural quarters', which are connected to both an historical remnant of migrant collectivism and commodification (Keith, 2005; Pugliese, 2007).

Global mobility continues and new populations enter cities, such that ethnicity continues to be a designation of importance for cities (McClinchey, 2008), both as 'enclaves' of consumption and 'enclaves' to be transformed into more palatable areas. In reference to Canada, Rankin and McLean (2015) contended that: 'celebrations of "diversity" and "multiculturalism" in creative city boosterism commodify difference and normalize processes of racialization through such practices as "ethnic packaging" and neighbourhood branding' (2015: 220–1).

This idea of branding hints at the multiple and overlapping spatialities of multicultural cities around forms of racialisation. For example, the idea of the 'enclave' is important for those that can be marketed in acceptable forms as legitimate, but some enclaves are those that are intelligible only as 'violent', 'dangerous' or in need of 'rebranding', for instance, the ghettos. As Leonardo and Hunter proposed: 'As an imagined space, the urban is constructed through multiple and often contradictory meanings' (Leonardo, 2009: 144). While Leonardo and Hunter are referring to the urban as primarily the inner city, the imagined space is equally applicable to those visions of suburbia (see also Dippo and James, 2011).

The growing power of culture in cities, both its commercialised and geographical power, has been identified in urban studies but less so in education. In talking about cultural spaces, Keith (2005) notes that the city is an important part of 'cultural dialogue'. He states that these spaces of 'contemporary urbanism can curate the presentation of ethnic difference and new forms of hybridity whilst simultaneously displacing appeals to community through processes of city transformation' (Keith, 2005: 113). Difference becomes tied to a commodity – such as restaurants – that communicate these differences in essentialised forms to the 'outside' world. In this way, the governance of the city is tied not just to incorporating the multiculture, but to the *creation* of racialisations and ethnicity for the subsequent commodification into gentrified markets (Comaroff and Comaroff, 2009).

We would suggest that there has never been a time when it was more urgent to avoid the concomitants of essentialising difference than our neoliberal present. And, there has never been a time when it has been more urgent to understand the politics of this, given the propensities of education to employ racialised school choice as a primary means of ostensibly implementing 'neoliberal educational equality'. The constant reinscription of difference, implicitly through city geographies and explicitly through school choice, substantially alters the cultural dialogue into simple forms of buying and selling difference.

Race and the challenge to the multicultural city

Race and space are contested and dynamic (Neely and Samura, 2011), unfolding in reference to contestation over schools in particular areas of cities, and in reference to particular bodies. As Mitchell posited: 'As a geographical project the co-production of race and space is never uncontested, and thus the spatiality of race often needs ordering and policing' (2000: 230). Keith's (2005) idea of place is useful for conceptualising 'places' as temporary achievements but, nonetheless, these temporary achievements are located geo-historically and are no more and no less moments of arbitrary closure. Hence, the subject, captured by the temporary achievements of race and place, constantly adapts, changes and becomes within the geographical politics of the city. Materially produced and with multiplied significations, 'a "place" in precise terms can have only a meaning of a particular moment' (Keith, 2005: 75). This is a moment of unequal encounter that is part of how 'cultural places' work with race, for in multicultural cities there is a tension 'between languages of belonging and forces of power that make racial subjects visible', and it is the city that 'is commonly crucial to the mediation of such tensions' (Keith, 2005: 6).

These relations are significant in that they indicate how place as event is tied up with the struggles over memory and histories of place, objects and encounters. As Dwyer and Bressey (2008) noted, a focus on a micropolitics of the city, on everyday encounters, has been a part of new geographies of race and ethnicity. One of the parts of this focus on these encounters is:

> some of the contradictions and conflicts which these intercultural or multicultural exchanges produce ... [This] also offers the possibility of understanding geographies of race and racism through 'extroverted' (Massey 1994) geographical imaginaries which re-entangle local experiences with transnational memories, networks and identifications. (Dwyer and Bressey, 2008: 5)

This is clear when schools are proposed and opened that carry with them an assemblage of geo-histories and racial prehensions – the very phenotype sensings that orient different bodies in different ways. The Africentric Alternative School is a trans-scalar event: an assemblage of Black education in Toronto, slavery and segregation in Canada, contestations over belonging in multicultural cities and nations, and so forth. This trans-scalar event, this assemblage, powerfully re-entangles and orients local experiences along with transnational memories and histories, powerfully shaping and reshaping the city.

Education policy, geo-history and some possible city futures

Soja (1996: 182–3) posited that 'a de-centering of the historical imagination ... works to un-learn its privilege and behave as it if is part of the margin, in a space-time or geohistory of radical openness'. Education policy in the city connects race and class, or more precisely for this chapter, schooling and economics are linked. The focus on the latter link means that education policy avoids anti-racist practices in favour of (the promise of) economic mobility within White markets. The latter simply extends the history of schooling as the economic engine of the biopolitical state. This time, however, it is aligned within the discourse of school enrolment problems, exacerbated by school-choice issues. Education policy, thus, depends on the racialised and marketised reconfiguring of space – that is, which parts of the city are deemed acceptable for the commodification and consumption of ethnicity.

For schools located in urban areas, where difference has been seen as a problem to be solved or occluded, there is a close coupling of the histories and geographies of schooling systems and cities; a school enters the domain not just of education but of how ideas of ethnicity may be constituted and marketed/branded within the city. There is an extensive racialised contestation over who has the right to define the parameters of the market, that is, which alternative schools are acceptable – and also a debate over who controls culture (Gilroy, 2000).

There is an imbrication of ethnicity, the city and education, particularly when ethnicity is understood as a value that is equivocated in the marketing of difference. Whether a principle of action or a testament to worth, ethnicity operates at least in two ways within the imbrications of the city and education. In the city a new school, while being located in a particular neighbourhood, has the capacity to travel across the city, and to bring to the fore questions of race and culture that are dealt with separately in other parts of the city through the commodification of difference. But when this idea of commodification is brought to bear on schooling, the multicultural city is unable to deal with difference; hence a new school disrupts, it disturbs, it possibly creates a new sense of the city.

FIVE

Difference and recognition

The shooting deaths of several young Black men between 1988 and 2007 were integral events in the becoming of the Africentric Alternative School. The shootings produced a spectrum of affects for those working to develop the school. This affective spectrum would coalesce with other feelings of empowerment and safety produced by the governing and patterned sequences of neoliberalism and biopolitics. This affective amalgam would serve as a powerful catalyst in the development of the school and in the fight against Black racism in Toronto more broadly.

Many initiatives from 1988 to 2007 were aimed at reducing anti-Black racism, including in the areas of educational and employment opportunities, policing behaviours, and through the creation of Ontario's Black Secretariat as the provincial means to support, coordinate and regulate these and other initiatives. Within these event-intervals, it is not hard to imagine several potential books that could examine in more detail police reform, non-discriminatory employment laws, and the rise and fall of the Black Secretariat as they influenced the becoming of the Africentric Alternative School. That is to say that the becoming of the Africentric Alternative School is only understandable within the truncated accounts of other events; series within series of entangled accounts related to police education, equal employment opportunities and governmental enforcement.

Our focus in this chapter is on the ways the becoming of the school entailed an established array of dispositifs concerned with recognition, difference, safety and 'identity politics'. These dispotifs had long but accessible histories within the city's educational programmes and provided the registers for thinking and acting for several trustees who would eventually cast votes on the fate of the school. The chapter discusses the politics of recognition in relation to broader anti-racist practices, and specifically discusses how these ideas were brought to bear upon the Toronto District School Board (TDSB) after the shooting and death of a grade nine student, Jordan Manners. We show how the shooting deaths of several Black men in Toronto were absorbed into policy regimes that affected the becoming of the school. Moreover, we show how impermanent ideas of recognition, representation and difference strongly steered policy making that ultimately produced the school.

The first part of this chapter traces the policy landscape that used and perpetuated these specific dispositifs, largely products of anti-racist literatures and ideas, and their concomitant effects (that is, 'identity politics'). The second half of the chapter traces how TDSB trustees used – and were used by – these dispositifs. The chapter illustrates how trustees altered these dispositifs in favour of the ascendant logics of economic and educational choice. Trustees were simultaneously constituted by the ensemble of anti-racist dispositifs, but in ways that accommodated and reinforced the policy mechanisms of educational choice and neoliberal ideas of freedom, understood as unfettered access to (quasi-) educational markets.

The safety of biopolitical recognition

As we identified in Chapter Two, the shooting death of a high school student Jordan Manners at C.W. Jefferys Collegiate Institute on 23 May 2007 led to renewed focus in Toronto on race and race-based statistics, and has been identified as a significant event in the becoming of the Africentric Alternative School (for example, Thompson and Wallner, 2011). As we noted, the shooting prompted the TDSB to address issues of race and racism, but framed within the existing and pervasive discourses of school safety and gun violence (with for example, the United States school shooting at Columbine as a precedent).

As a response, the board formed the School Community Safety Advisory Panel (SCSAP), convened with the goal of understanding Manners' death (see School Community Safety Advisory Panel, 2008, also known as the *Falconer report*). This tragic event extended and entangled the histories of young Black men, gun violence and school safety. The net effect of this entanglement further shaped the Africentric Alternative School as a kind of safe haven, a sanctuary. In addition to ideas of neoliberal choice and biopolitical equality, the becoming of the school was now enunciated as a symbol of hope amid the violence of anti-Black racism.

On 5 June 2007, SCSAP ended its investigation and, in its report tabled at the TDSB on 10 January 2008, it concluded that school safety was primarily a product of recognition and difference. More precisely, unsafe schools were the result of not recognising difference. The report proposed re-engaging strategies that accommodated the unique circumstances of marginalised students and those with complex needs through social services support, along with an inclusive curriculum targeting their realities. Underlying these ideas, the SCSAP appealed to a broader ethos and stated that:

> the notion of equity ... has, as its most fundamental tenet, the *recognition* that people's *differences* are to be recognized and accounted for with a view to creating environments that do not push people out. Strategies geared towards inclusion involve adopting approaches and programs meant to recognize and acknowledge the diversity of the student population. (SCSAP, 2008: 7, emphasis added)

Ideas of recognition* and difference were integral ways to map the becoming of the Africentric school. In addition to the material affordances the school would provide, therefore, the becoming of the school was marked as an aspiration; an aspiration to counter feelings of being unsafe, and of disillusionment and self-loss. Such a cartography provides a tracing of how the school operated as a beacon of hope alongside the eternal recurrence of police reform, (un)equal employment opportunities, limited access to housing and health care, and a litany of bureaucratic attempts at social equity. In other words, the becoming of the school was quickly subsumed within the circular dispositifs of social equity practices performed in the city of Toronto.

The figure of the 'child' in need of protection would be a relatively new addition to the ensemble of dispositifs circulating and regulating anti-racist attempts. While the *Falconer report* (SCSAP, 2008) did not make reference to initiatives like the Africentric Alternative School, subsequent TDSB reports would position the school within different discourses of equity, recognition and difference that were accepted by and enunciated by the SCSAP. A school premised on Black racialisations would align with the recognition of difference that the SCSAP endorsed, or so it appeared.

Yonge Street riot

Jordan Manners' death in 2007 was different than, or perhaps extended, the history of anti–Black violence in Toronto in at least two ways. First, Manners' death was not the result of police force and, second, the shooting occurred in a school. The net effect of this particular shooting was fear about the spread of anti–Black racism (that is, beyond policing), which merged with existing fears about guns and school violence. As we noted, Manners' death could position the recommendation for the Africentric Alternative School as a respite and/or solution to the affective assemblage of feeling unsafe, angry and disillusioned, with a griping sense of disempowerment. The TDSB would seize upon notions of recognition and difference, as discussed in SCSAP, as part of the policy rationale for, and marketing of, the school.

The shooting death of Jordan Manners was not a singular, or what is commonly referred to as an 'isolated', event. Events are never isolated, but they are often framed in the singular to obfuscate or deny the in/compossibles that produce events. For instance, it is much easier to believe in a singular and 'spontaneous' moment rather than to try and understand the histories, intensities and extensions of anti-Black racism. The singular is a clever dispositif that reproduces power arrangements. As singular and tragic as Manners' death was to his immediate family and friends, nevertheless, his death was yet another in a series of shooting deaths of young Black men in Toronto.

The Yonge Street riot was, in many ways, the release of mounting anger in the late 1980s about the way the Toronto police were handling their interactions with minority youngsters (Black Canadians in particular). The fatal shootings of Lester Donaldson on 9 August 1988 in Toronto, and Michael Wade Lawson (a teenager) four months later, mobilised Ontario's Black community into action. Two days before the riot, demonstrations were organised in reaction to the police shooting of 22-year-old Jamaican immigrant Raymond Lawrence, the eighth Black man shot in four years, and the fourth fatal shooting. The courts would later acquit police who were involved in the 1988 shooting death of Lawson.

The riot followed a major protest organised by the Black Defence Action Committee (BDAC) which gathered outside the United States consulate. The location was chosen to protest the acquittals of the four police officers in the Rodney King beating, which sparked the riots in Los Angeles that had occurred the week before. The main concern of those who assembled was the perceived racism on the part of the Metro Toronto police force. The BDAC protest would eventually give rise to a Task Force on Race Relations and Policing initiated by the Solicitor General of Ontario in December 1988. A year later, the Task Force would produce a report (Lewis et al., 1989) that a concluded that visible racial minorities believed they were policed unfairly and were denied the opportunity to participate in law enforcement and crime prevention in their own community. This highlighted that, for the Black community, policy was not a democratic mechanism to pursue and uphold liberties; rather, it was used as a tactic to delay the redress of racial discrimination.

Among its recommendations, the Task Force on Race Relations and Policing identified establishing a community-based monitoring and audit board, with a defined anti-racist component to eradicate systemic barriers to treating Black people equally in police policies, practices and procedures (Lewis et al., 1989). The Task Force also recommended establishing committees with community and police representatives to advise on the integration of race-relations and anti-racism content in police training programmes (Lewis et al., 1989). The report further recommended revising the police preparation curriculum at all levels, in order to foster racial and cultural understanding, tolerance and recognition of cultural difference, based on intercultural frameworks (Lewis et al., 1989).

Despite the report's 57 recommendations on police monitoring, race-relations education, use of force and community relations, the Black community continued to experience systematic discrimination and to be treated unequally by criminal justice institutions. For many, this fact, coupled with Lawrence's shooting and the acquittal of police officers involved in race-based brutality, triggered what became known as the Yonge Street riot.

Towards a new beginning

Then-Premier Bob Rae would appoint Stephen Lewis to report on the state of race relations across the province after the Yonge Street riot. Lewis identified 'anti-Black racism' as the main cause underlying the riot (Lewis, 1992: 2). After meeting with many members of the Black community, Lewis concluded that the Black community was subjected to 'systemic discrimination', which led to a significantly disadvantaged and vulnerable social position within Toronto (1992: 2).

Many of the report's recommendations dealt with the police, and suggested the creation of a systematic audit of police race-relations policies across the province, the intensification of race-relations training and the investigation of racism in other sectors of the criminal justice system, including the judiciary and detention centres (Lewis, 1992: 4-16). Moreover, the report recommended the prompt implementation of employment equity legislation, the upgrading of the Ontario Anti-Racism Secretariat, the creation of a Cabinet Committee on Race Relations to meet with members of minority communities on a regular basis, and funding for community development projects to address the social and economic issues within communities (1992: 31-33).

Although a timeline published by the *Toronto Star* considered that 'Stephen Lewis's public probe in the wake of the Yonge Street Riots

... [supported] the idea of black-focused schools', there were no specific references to such schools within the body of the text or the recommendations (*Toronto Star*, 18 November 2007). Instead, Lewis proposed the reformation of curricula at every level to align them with multicultural and anti-racism education principles and contents, and recommended the elimination of streaming or ability tracking in schools (1992: 25).

Alongside Stephen Lewis's report (1992), representatives from the four levels of government, and the Black Canadian community formed a working group to address the concerns of the Black Canadian community in Metropolitan Toronto. Two representatives from each level of government formed the working group, plus seven prominent members of the African Canadian community, including Thando Hyman, who would eventually serve as the first school principal of the Africentric Alternative School.

Set up in the aftermath of the riots on Yonge Street in May 1992, this working group developed a report proposing the creation of a Black-focused school in Toronto. A key link between ideas of recognition and difference, and the becoming of the Africentric Alternative School, was the idea of 'Black-focused schools' outlined in the policy document *Towards a new beginning* (Ontario Government/African Canadian Community Working Group, 1992).

The working group met with a cross-section of Toronto's Black community, with special attention given to highlighting problems facing youth. Based on their inquiries, the working group formulated an integrated and strategic plan of action to address the systematic racial discrimination and its effects.

The education system was designed to play an essential role in this process: the working group proposed the creation of 'focused schools' as a short-term strategy seeking to improve the self-esteem of Black youth. The working group proposed that Black-focused schools would foster a better understanding and appreciation of the historical contributions of the Black Community to Canadian society and, by so doing, would help Black Canadian youth to reach their 'full potential' within the system. The report proposed that one predominantly Black junior high school in each of Metro's six municipalities should become a pilot Black-focused institution, with compulsory Black history and culture courses taught, and an increase in Black teaching staff at each location.

Fallout from *Towards a new beginning*

The Black-focused school pilot initiative received mixed reactions from the community. According to a *Toronto Star* article (14 December 1992), the proposal drew criticism from numerous Black Canadians who regarded it as a step back to the days of segregation. For instance, Wilson Head, a retired York University professor and an influential member of the Black community, said the idea smacked of segregation. 'I went through that,' said the Atlanta-born Head, who would pass away less than a year later. 'None of us believed that we were as good as schools with white children' (Rankin, 1992). Given the multicultural nature of Canada's society, he posited, Black children needed to learn with White kids and children of other colours, not separated from them.

In response to the criticisms, John Dennison, chair of the working group, argued that the proposal was about 'integration', not segregation (Rankin, 1992). In his view, other schools should emulate some of the proposed ideas (such as increasing coverage of Black history in the curriculum, providing anti-racism education for teachers, fostering community-based relationships and school clubs for other ethnic groups). Anne-Marie Stewart, another author of the document, believed Black-focused schools were a long overdue approach to tackle the systemic problems facing Black students in Toronto schools. In her view, this type of school would 'draw black people together at certain schools' (Rankin, 1992). Extending Dennison's point, Stewart argued that achieving integration among Black youth through Black-focused schools was a necessary step before attempting integration with any other culture.

Similarly, educational psychologist Ralph Agard defended the report, saying that segregation was never intended in the proposal and it should not produce fear (Rankin, 1992). As an example, he alleged that a separate school system already existed for the Catholic Church and they received government funding. The idea that separate schools already existed would be a factor for several TDSB trustees 15 years later, as they wrestled with the criteria that were used to establish notions of difference and recognition for the Africentric Alternative School.

Lloyd McKell, at that time community services officer for the Toronto Board of Education, was supportive of the Black-focused school initiative, providing students of other backgrounds would not be denied access to this type of school. In his view, Black children and youth would benefit from studying in a 'learning environment where [Black students] can see black teachers, black school office staff, books dealing with black history and culture, pictures on the wall of black heroes that they can identify with' (Rankin, 1992). Moreover, McKell considered this type of school would provide something that was clearly missing in the mainstream system for many Black Canadian students: a Black-focused curriculum, which was inclusive of their particular heritage as Black students.

Critics of the working group's pilot proposal argued that the existence of Black-focused schools would take the pressure off non-Black schools to revise their Eurocentric curriculum. Furthermore, critics feared that focused schools would alienate non-Black students, and erode whatever little integration that had occurred by attracting Black students from local schools. As such, critics argued that Black-focused schools would essentially create an all-Black school through de facto policies of choice, a move that ignored the way White, middle-class parents, even in the early days of policy-led school choice, had mobilised to ensure that their children only went to school with 'people like us'. In the early 1990s, the logics and rationales of nascent educational markets were already in play and used to provide counter arguments against the development of Black-focused schools.

Policy ambivalence

According to the *Toronto Star*, the final agenda item on the Toronto Metro Council meeting for 6 January 1993 was the *Towards a new beginning* report. Scarborough Councillor Brian Harrison presented the motion to 'receive' the report, which in effect was a motion of no action. Only 21 of the 35 Metro councillors were in the room, and Harrisonss motion was carried by 13 to 8. Harrison explained his motion by stating that, '[t]he report recommends special economic help for black businessmen and, reading between the lines, it sounds like they want money for a cultural centre and even segregated schools. I don't believe people would support all that special treatment' (Lewis Stein, 1993).

Metro chair Alan Tonks expressed his concern about this result by arguing he was afraid 'people in the black community will interpret this as meaning that we have abandoned our commitment to fight against racism. And that is just not true' (Lewis Stein, 1993). He gave assurances that Metro would carry on with its anti-racism programme while attempting to have the report reconsidered. Likewise, Ken Jeffers, a co-author of *Towards a new beginning*, expressed his disappointment, noting that not one Metro school board (prior to the creation of the TDSB) had developed a Black-focused junior high school. On 4 May 1993, Jeffers and co-panellists on the African Canadian Community

Working Group reported back to a public meeting about progress – or lack thereof – since the Yonge Street riot. As Jeffers sadly put it '[t]he anniversary brings questions. It is just as we said – nobody's going to do anything' (Wright, 1993).

According to Lewinberg (1999), none of the proposed 13 'Action Steps' of the report were acted upon. He claimed, '[s]ix months after the riot the heat was off and with the provincial government moving ahead with several initiatives, federal and municipal governments could afford to stay clear' (1999: 201). Metro Councillor Olivia Chow asserted that no real change had taken place in Metro, and the funding was allocated to law enforcement instead of the measures recommended in the report.

At the provincial level, Stephen Lewis, who in his June 1992 report urged the province to revamp the education system to reflect multicultural changes in Ontario, was 'disappointed that things haven't happened on that front' (Wright, 1993). Despite the lack of progress in reforming the education system along the lines of Stephen Lewis's report, the New Democratic Party government attempted to address mounting calls for reform by launching the Royal Commission on Learning in May 1993 to conduct an overall review of public education, the first review since the Hope Commission in 1950 (Gidney, 1999; Anderson and Jaafar, 2003). According to Anderson and Jaafar (2003: 9), this initiative constituted a political attempt to engage the public in mapping the future of Ontario education, 'after the government's initial policy agenda failed to win much public support'.

Another policy attempt

The Royal Commission on Learning was a broad assessment of education policy and practice in Ontario. While it too would provide another lengthy list of recommendations that were not acted upon, the commission would enunciate similar ideas about recognition and difference in relation to Black-focused schools. The commission's report recommended that:

> in jurisdictions with large numbers of black students, school boards, academic authorities, faculties of education and representatives of the black community collaborate to establish demonstration schools and innovative programs based on best practices in bringing about academic success for black students. (Begin et al., 1994: 178)

The idea of demonstration schools was not sufficiently detailed, much like the idea of pilot schools discussed in Chapter Two. Nevertheless, Black-demonstration schools resonated with the notion of Black-focused schools discussed in the *Towards a new beginning* report, and maintain similar logics of difference and recognition.

The recommendations of the commission would ultimately wither after the New Democratic Party lost the provincial election in 1995 to the Conservative Party. Ideas of recognition, difference and Black-focused schools would lie dormant until Angela Wilson revived these ideas nearly ten years later, when they would be reinterpreted through the neoliberal logics and rationales of educational choice and self-separation (as discussed in Chapter Three).

The appropriation of anti-racist discourse into economic principles would prove to be a successful strategy, as the Africentric Alternative School would open its doors in September 2009. However, the appropriation of anti-racist discourse into economic principles would ignite a maelstrom of 'identity politics' within different racialised communities leading up to the school's opening. The next section illustrates how different Board Trustees and various educational activists enacted the dispositifs of recognition and difference within the ascendent logics of neoliberal educational choice.

The politics of educational recognition

The ideas of recognition and difference were coded within education policy prior to the report from SCSAP, *Towards a new beginning* or the report of the Royal Commission on Learning. The Africentric Alternative School utilised this multicultural history of recognition and difference through its relation to historic formations of prior ethnic-specific schools, namely First Nation schooling, Catholic schooling and French immersion schooling in the 1970s and 1980s. One trustee waxed lyrically about the Africentric Alternative School, and stated, '[t]he old Toronto Board of Education had what was originally called the Wandering Spirit School, and is now called First Nation School, which does have a curriculum that I guess you would call First Nation-centric' (Interview). Another trustee reminded us about Canada's Catholic school system in relation to the Africentric Alternative School. She stated, 'And don't forget, we have a publicly funded Catholic separate system to begin with' (Interview).

An education activist in Toronto noted that discussions about difference and recognition in schooling were difficult conversations, particularly due to the kinds of histories associated with ethnic and linguistic identifications. She sardonically stated: 'And it's a very hard conversation because you actually have to bring French immersion into it too. French immersion parents are way scarier [politically adept] than any other parents' (Interview). Another trustee informed us that 'There are lots of Jewish schools in Toronto, but they're private' (Interview). Historical Jewish schools amplified the dispositifs of difference and recognition in Toronto, in the sense that they have been precedents of culturally focused schools, though have been private with no public funding. Trustees also remarked upon private Islamic schools that were seen either as 'safe havens' or 'religious ghettos' (for example, Zine, 2007).

The Africentric Alternative School, then, was conceived alongside rationales of equity that posited difference and recognition as acceptable forms of cultural politics within the old Toronto Board of Education (the previous amalgamated board), within which all other alternative schools had been located. These schools included the Wandering Spirit School, and the establishment and short life of a 25-student Black-focused programme called Nighana within a school in 1994 (McGaskell, 2005), the latter the closest Toronto would come to a Black-focused school prior to the Africentric Alternative School.

The Africentric Alternative School quickly became entangled within a set of policy enactments concerning several 'schools of recognition' (as we might call them) that the TDSB proposed around the same time (circa 2005), including schools enacted on the basis of gender, sexuality and high-performing physical ability (athletes). Historical orders of multicultural representation in Canada – coupled with an intensive neoliberal agenda in the board to marketise schools – provided a rapid increase in the enactments of several schools of recognition. Interestingly, there was an increasing anticipation, or fear, about the becoming of a Muslim-centric school based on ideas of recognition and difference (see Figure 5.1). Figure 5.1 arranges the overlapping talk of five trustees as they grappled with ideas of difference, recognition and educational equity.

Figure 5.1: The dispositifs of difference, recognition and choice in the TDSB

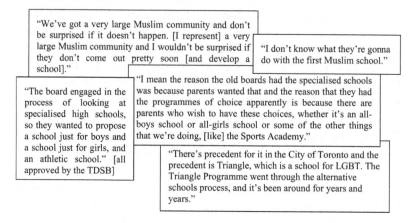

"We've got a very large Muslim community and don't be surprised if it doesn't happen. [I represent] a very large Muslim community and I wouldn't be surprised if they don't come out pretty soon [and develop a school]."

"I don't know what they're gonna do with the first Muslim school."

"The board engaged in the process of looking at specialised high schools, so they wanted to propose a school just for boys and a school just for girls, and an athletic school." [all approved by the TDSB]

"I mean the reason the old boards had the specialised schools was because parents wanted that and the reason that they had the programmes of choice apparently is because there are parents who wish to have these choices, whether it's an all-boys school or all-girls school or some of the other things that we're doing, [like] the Sports Academy."

"There's precedent for it in the City of Toronto and the precedent is Triangle, which is a school for LGBT. The Triangle Programme went through the alternative schools process, and it's been around for years and years."

The ideas of safety and violence were key catalysts in the becomings of culturally focused schools in the TDSB. While the Sports Academy falls somewhat outside these registers (as do many of the 44 choice schools in the TDSB), the Africentric Alternative School, First Nation School, Triangle, and the Boys and Girls Academies all utilised the ideas of safety and violence as part of the rationale for their respective becomings in the TDSB school market. One trustee noted that he and his fellow trustees 'used a model to separate students' through ideas of difference, recognition and alternative school policies to produce school sanctuaries, embedded within the existing (quasi) school market. Over time, however, trustees noted a commodifying effect produced from these market enactments. A trustee remarked:

'So one of the things that came out of that [school-choice deliberation] was a discussion amongst a number of us about "so what do we do now because we're making things worse." And, out of the Boys schools and the Girls schools, those who were deeply opposed to the Africentric school were equally deeply opposed to Boys and Girls schools. It was about identity. I'm not sure the others would articulate it quite the same way. But I believe we all have the same core fear.' (Interview)

Additional remarks confirmed that trustees worried about the possibility that the school-choice market would provide additional commodifications of difference for enterprising cultural groups within the board. For instance:

'I understand the focus because it's an Africentric curriculum so it's a focused curriculum which is different from a traditional school. However, there are lots of specialty schools that require focused curriculums, you know, are not called focus schools. And, what's the difference between specialty, boutique, focus, choice? The choice thing is a big deal. Lots of people are really wanting to move away from that term because they don't want to have charter schools because of all the problems that are associated with those.' (Interview)

Finally, trustees worried that their support for recognition, difference and school choice would produce an amalgam that would ultimately erode any democratic function of schooling. One trustee put it this way:

'[in] kindergarten we have books about two-mother families and two-father families. And we periodically have deep community outrage over the use of those books because it goes very much against parental teaching ... [Those that oppose the books] would love to have their own schools. [But then] [t]he Sunnis and Shias wouldn't share their schools, the Ismailis wouldn't share the schools, the Sufis wouldn't, right, so there'd be the guys from Afghanistan, the guys from Pakistan, their different languages, they'd have their own schools, we'd have schools and schools and schools and schools ...' (Interview)

This trustee extrapolated the logics of recognition and difference into a kind of infinite regression of various identities, albeit apparently produced in their shared outrage against lesbian and gay parenting. Notwithstanding the liberties taken in the construction of the extrapolation, the idea that difference is an infinite regression – even within periodic intersections – produced a crisis within board governance. Interestingly, the trustee ruminations did not indicate any thoughts about the potential markets that might be produced in the name of difference's infinite regressions, perhaps conceived of as 'future market niches'. This absence of entrepreneurial thought, or perhaps that the cost of new markets was too high for Toronto education, was consistent within the board, even though the board shared concerns about the quickly eroding multicultural ethos produced from upholding unfettered access to the board's quasi-school markets.

Policy subjects

The preceding policy landscape of school choice, alternative schooling and identity politics, positioned trustees politically in relation to the becoming of the Africentric Alternative School. Moreover, this landscape affected how trustees were treated in relation to the school. Here, the becoming of the school ordered and patterned the actions of supporters and opponents respectively. The most significant force that patterned actions was the definition and identification of 'Black'.

Figure 5.2: The politics of Blackness

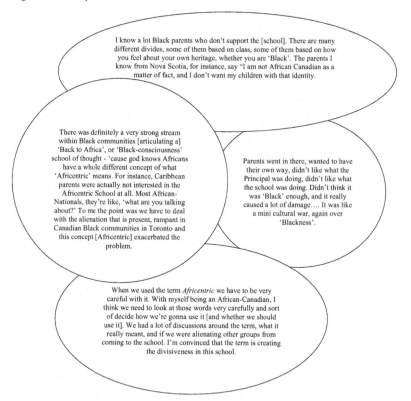

I know a lot Black parents who don't support the [school]. There are many different divides, some of them based on class, some of them based on how you feel about your own heritage, whether you are 'Black'. The parents I know from Nova Scotia, for instance, say "I am not African Canadian as a matter of fact, and I don't want my children with that identity.

There was definitely a very strong stream within Black communities [articulating a] 'Back to Africa', or 'Black-consciousness' school of thought - 'cause god knows Africans have a whole different concept of what 'Africentric' means. For instance, Caribbean parents were actually not interested in the Africentric School at all. Most African-Nationals, they're like, 'what are you talking about?' To me the point was we have to deal with the alienation that is present, rampant in Canadian Black communities in Toronto and this concept [Africentric] exacerbated the problem.

Parents went in there, wanted to have their own way, didn't like what the Principal was doing, didn't like what the school was doing. Didn't think it was 'Black' enough, and it really caused a lot of damage.... It was like a mini cultural war, again over 'Blackness'.

When we used the term *Africentric* we have to be very careful with it. With myself being an African-Canadian, I think we need to look at those words very carefully and sort of decide how we're gonna use it [and whether we should use it]. We had a lot of discussions around the term, what it really meant, and if we were alienating other groups from coming to the school. I'm convinced that the term is creating the divisiveness in this school.

The becoming of the school, specifically the preconditions of biopolitics, neoliberalism, the ideas and registers of difference and recognition, and the city itself, influenced people's political action. In this sense, these preconditions affected people's behaviour rather than the assumed idea that people were influencing the event. Instances of physical threats and physical violence were noted by some trustees when they questioned assumptions that connected the school to identity, difference and recognition (including trustees who voted in favour of the school). One trustee stated:

> 'I've gotten so many threats on my life because I didn't support the school. I remember one night very clearly: a woman came up and she made the sign of a gun and said "you should be fucking shot." Another time, I was about to leave to go down the stairs and she pushed me. The security guard was behind me, so he had the hood of my coat to pull me back or I would have gone right down on my face.' (Interview)

Another trustee stated, 'phone call after phone call, and email after email. People were furious, angry, sad, and hateful. I started getting threats. I got a couple death threats. I got a lot of hate mail' (Interview). Questioning the dispositifs of difference and recognition was difficult for trustees because it was fraught with danger, depending on where one is located upon the unequal and historical playing-field of identifications (that is, gender, sexuality, class, race and so on), and expected to be an advocate according to an identity category. For instance, a trustee who voted against the school ironically stated, 'Everybody hates me, everybody dislikes me, yes I'm a traitor, I'm a sell-out to the Black race.'

Summary

This chapter focused on the ways *difference* and *recognition* were enacted by policy actors, and specifically though educational policy in ways that were not divorced from neoliberal policy practices: school choice, school markets and ethnic commodifications. Indeed, the Africentric Alternative School depended on economic ideas to articulate notions of educational difference and recognition, which subsequently performed policy subjects and enacted (and cemented) school markets. Trustees, then, enacted policy within a complex and politically dangerous ensemble of dispositifs that performed specific policy enactments around phenotype identifications, recognitions of shifting signifiers (that is, cultural belongings or 'Blackness'), and a rapidly growing and changing school market that required commodified brands in order to advertise difference through the auspices of choice.

The impossibilities of representation

Recognition

*Perhaps no other statement represents the contemporary multicultural politics of recognition better than Charles Taylor's (1994: 27) that:

> our identity is partly shaped by recognition or its absence, often misrecognition of others, and so a person or group of people can suffer real damage, real distortion, if the people or society mirror back to them a confining or demeaning or contemptible picture of themselves.

Taylor's statement locates ideas of recognition within representations of people and groups that align – or not – with ideas of identity. In other words, Taylor's statement describes a process whereby the validity of the recognition is determined by a correspondence theory of truth. Correspondence theories rely on personal and/or group characteristics (which need to be specified) that relate to some aspect of reality (which also needs to be specified). However, Taylor does not specify how the processes of correspondence take place; he simply asserts the processes with allusions to image circulation and notions about the validity of interpretations.

Taylor's contributions about recognitive multicultural politics are supported through ideas about metaphysical realism, whereby objects in the world exist independently of thought, and the respective natures or essences of objects are independent from how these objects are conceived (and for our purposes, how these objects are perceived). This metaphysical realism is another reason we examine the ontologies involved with the becoming of the school (and see Chapter One for an overview of how we are using ontology in this book). As we noted in in the introductory chapter, we can posit the processes of mis/recognition in reference to Canadian multiculturalism in at least three ways. First, multiculturalism can be an institutional strategy for governments to manage and control difference. Strategically, multiculturalism:

> allows the state to set the terms of the 'difference debate'. These terms are highly individual: they are concerned with individual rights and preferences – the right to choose and display difference with respect to individual identity. (Mitchell, 2003: 391)

Institutionally, multiculturalism permits 'minority' groups to be included, as long as they follow certain carefully prescribed rules about how this is to be undertaken. Judith Butler noted that '[t]his becomes especially acute for those who can only enter the existing structures of political representation by assuming a position as a subject that actually effaces their historical and cultural history and agency' (Willig, 2012: 141).

Second, mis/recognition is evident in Canadian multiculturalism when it practises 'colour-blind' notions that occlude race and and racism altogether (Mackey, 1999). This means, 'for the most part, education in Canada is mired in a color-blind and monocultural discourse in terms of vision, content and style so that the promise of democracy, inclusivity and equity continues to elude minority students' (James, 2011: 192). This particular process accounts for the naïve substitution of a concerted racial politics by what we are calling in a contemporary sense, 'All Lives Matter'.

Market forms of education, such as school choice, account for the third way to understand mis/recognitions of Canadian multiculturalism. This occurs when identities are articulated and recognised in education markets as a corrective to 'colour-blind' multiculturalism. Hale (2005: 28) stated that the same:

> collective rights, granted as compensatory measures to 'disadvantaged' cultural groups, are an integral part of neoliberal ideology. These distinctive cultural policies (along with their sociopolitical counterparts), rather than simply the temporal lapse between classic liberalism and its latter day incarnation, are what give the 'neo' its real meaning. To emphasize the integral relationship between these new cultural rights and neoliberal political economic reforms, I use the term 'neoliberal multiculturalism.'

Neoliberal multiculturalism is a seductive form of recognition that sits within a 'framework in which the subject can only become a subject as such through being recognized by another as a subject' (Grosz, 2002: 465).

Furthermore, neoliberal multiculturalism is a form that neglects Fraser's (1999 1995) assertion that 'justice today requires *both* redistribution and recognition'. However, neoliberal multiculturalism does not redistribute through its recognitive powers; it simply perpetuates the 'decoupling' of cultural politics from social politics (Fraser, 1999).

Phenotype codes

The three registers of Canadian multiculturalism all relate to the ways representations are cast. However, these registers do not account for how these representations are recognised; albeit these registers attempt to code interpretations in ways that align with notions of ontological (that is, metaphysical) validity. Gilroy (2000: 179) observed that the production of representations is often placed in the hands of cultural absolutists who treat difference as a: 'piece of intellectual property over which they alone hold effective copyright. Their expositions of it specify the elusive qualities of racialized difference that only they can claim to be able to comprehend and to paraphrase, if not exactly decode.'

Phenotype difference has been used historically as a way to infer cultural identifications from biology. Racial phenotypes operate as signs of biological identity, indeed genetic destiny, and express variations within different hierarchies (for example, intellect, behaviour, educational attainment and so on). Inferred identities are used to legitimate various eugenic projects, but also, and germane to this book, to legitimate various social equity attempts to establish social equity via recognition. Racial phenotypes similarly function in important ways within discussions of difference. Racial phenotypes are ways to distinguish non-White people from White, and in so doing, produce a racial hierarchy even when racial phenotypes are used to compare two non-White groups.

However, race and racial phenotypes are better understood as constitutive of multiple relations of power, given the lack of evidence linking phenotypes to particular effects. As Amin (2010: 7) posits: 'racial practice becomes an everyday "doing", well before thought, effortlessly weaving together historically honed folk summaries of others that people carry in their heads and a phenomenology of bodily response that also recurs with uncanny consistency'.

Racial phenotypes, understood as socially constituted and constituting rather than metaphysically real, alter how these signs function within different registers of recognition. As floating signifiers, racial phenotypes dramatically alter notions of recognition that assume accurate perceptions and authentic representations.

Thus, socially constitutive phenotypes are often tasked with accompanying exercises that try to determine the veracity of racialised signs within different registers, as in 'being true' to one's race. For instance, a cornucopia of metaphors has emerged as way to express the veracity of different phenotype representations and performances. The 'banana' or 'Twinkie' (Asian), the 'Oreo' (Black), the 'coconut' (Brown, Latino/a) and the 'apple' (Indigenous or Native

American) are the names for those whose White interiors, through overtly performative acts, betray their exterior phenotypes/black. The nature of race as socially and bodily constituted invokes additional registers in which recognition takes place. These additional registers – codings and decodings – are enacted in order to define the ontologies of people. In other words, Judith Butler noted that 'there are schemes of recognition that determine in a relative sense who will be regarded as a subject worthy of recognition' (Willig, 2012: 141).

The absence of recognisability jeopardises life, and hence the registers and schemes of recognition are activities concerned with the biopolitical.

Difference

The idea of difference is implicated within ideas of recognition. This point may seem obvious, in that difference is perceived in some way; however, the relationships between difference and recognition are not so obvious and have proven decidedly problematic in education, and particularly in equity attempts through education policy.

Difference makes distinctions between things (states, conditions, people) that are assumed to be equivalent or identical in some way. Difference is also used to illustrate distinctions over a period of time, often referred to as change or variation. In either case, difference refers to variations between groupings and requires processes of comparison (Stagoll, 2010).

The assumptions of equivalence that underlie most conceptions of difference produce discourses of identity and identification. Equivalence or identity is often considered a stable property or essence of things, and can be developed by subsuming variation through aggregates or arithmetical means. Moreover, processes of comparison (and there are many) that premise difference also produce discourses of recognition and representation.

That is, in order to identify difference, it must be perceived, intuited or affirmed in some way. Through processes of recognition, the identification of difference becomes a substantial epistemological project. In education, the identification of difference is a major impetus that organises and arranges schooling, for example in Toronto, and the conflation of bodies, identity and a school, and the collecting of race-based statistics. The practices of tracking, streaming or grouping students' differences reveal a predominant form of thinking within schooling. So much so, that Baker (2002) noted how this kind of thinking had translated into predatory behaviour by educators when attempting to identify difference in schools.

Difference, then, is an idea of exteriority that is buttressed by the various means of developing and/or recognising distinctions, whereas notions of identity lie buried within ideas of metaphysical realism (for example, genetics) and/or underpinning structures of socially constitutive processes (for example, sociology). Paul Gilroy (2000) illustrated (in the following long quote) how racial identities continue to function as a strategy for equity attempts, but one with severe limitations. Gilroy stated:

> Identity is latent destiny. Seen or unseen, on the surface of the body or buried deep in its cells, identity forever sets one group apart from others who lack the particular, chosen traits that become the basis of typology and comparative evaluation. No longer a site for the affirmation of subjectivity and autonomy, identity mutates. Its motion reveals a deep desire for mechanical solidarity, seriality, and hypersimilarity. The scope for individual agency dwindles and then disappears. People become bearers of the differences that the rhetoric of absolute identity invents and then invites them to celebrate. Rather than communicating and making choices, individuals are seen as obedient, silent passengers moving across a flattened moral landscape toward the fixed destinies to which their their essential identities, their genes, and the closed cultures they create have consigned them once and for all. And yet, the desire to fix identity in the body is inevitably frustrated by the body's refusal to disclose the required signs of absolute incompatibility people imagine to be located there.

Difference-in-itself

There is a small, perhaps esoteric, literature that discusses difference without assuming equivalence, and hence, produces a very different understanding of identity and recognition; that is difference without identity as 'difference-in-itself' (Deleuze, 1991, 1994). In this literature, difference is asserted as a perennial condition, whereas groupings of equivalence or identity are impossible because difference, by default, constantly alters, changes or is a process that is 'in effect' or 'in duration'.

Deleuze (1991: 23) observed that positing difference that presumes an identity as a sufficient cause (rather than contingent effect) is a 'difference by degree'. Deleuze (1991: 23) distinguished 'difference by degree' with *difference in kind*; whereas the latter marks the endless qualitative differences that resist categorisation. Deleuze (1994) claimed that difference by degree is ultimately reduced to 'difference in kind' when assumptions of identity are examined.

Deleuze (1994: 138, original emphasis) argued that, '*difference* [by degree] *becomes an object of representation always in relation to a conceived identity, a judged analogy, and imagined opposition or a perceived similitude*'. In this sense, 'difference by degree' is a perception applied as a difference *between* (things, objects, states, people and so on) and involves grouping things that are purportedly the same and noting distinctions between them.

Initially, and in contrast to 'difference between', we might consider 'difference within' as a way to understand *difference-in-itself*. In order to compare, 'difference by degree' invokes universals or transcendent understandings (for example, standards, aggregates, identities) to denote coherent and different classifications. 'Signification' is the term Deleuze used to refer to the representations between transcendental concepts and particular objects, which in turn, produces a politics of representation.

'Difference-in-itself' is an idea that does not presuppose identities. Instead, 'difference-in-itself' is an affirmation of the 'singularity' of each moment, thing, state and so on, a 'particularity that is' and an 'indetermination, newness which creates itself' (Deleuze, 1994: 48). 'Difference-in-itself' extends the idea of distinctions to the point where notions of 'the same' or 'identity' are seriously questioned, if not entirely dismissed. Deleuze (1994: 225) would argue that 'difference-in-itself' 'does not negate difference: on the contrary, it recognizes difference just enough to affirm that it negates itself, given sufficient extensity and time'.

Here, 'difference-in-itself' assumes an 'intensive multiplicity' that is constantly produced by indeterminacies and chance. Difference, then, is rearticulated as the constant changes in a singularity that are constantly becoming and not able to be grouped or organised in relation to universals or transcendentals.

Édouard Glissant (1989) and his version of 'creolization' is an important illustration of 'difference-in-itself' (and particularly germane in its location of the Caribbean as a contrasting signification of African 'Black' in this study). Rejecting hybridity and intersectionality, two areas that have been key parts of identity research in education, Glissant argued that creolisation was a process of constant becoming, and specifically a creative becoming away from fixed identities and towards states of constant flux. Glissant (1989:140) argued:

> creolization demonstrates that henceforth it is no longer valid to glorify 'unique' origins that the race safeguards and prolongs ... To assert that people are creolized, that creolization has value is to deconstruct in this

way the category of 'creolized' that is considered a half way between two 'pure' extremes.

Glissant rearticulates hybrid notions of creolisations by operationalising 'difference-in-itself' in order to demarcate a becoming 'into another people' that experience 'the constantly shifting and variable process of creolization (of relationship, or relativity)' (1989: 15). For our purposes, Glissant's ideas about creolisation are examples of how 'difference by degree' is challenged through his rejection of identity based on 'uniqueness' and 'purity'.

'New' forms of equity

Notwithstanding Deleuze's and Glissant's examples of 'difference-in-itself', the possibility of asserting *difference-in-itself* is part of a cultural politics in education that is precarious, and for some (including the trustees in our study) life-threatening. In claiming *difference-in-itself* as both an analytic and as a political possibility, dangers of radical exclusion lie beneath attempts at de/identifying – which we note are risks that are disproportionately assumed – if at all – depending on different and unequal social arrangements. For example, Étienne Balibar (2005: 28) noted how presumptions of identity, and disavowal of the same presumptions, run serious risks of radical exclusions. He stated:

> An assertion of singularity, differing from any type, is an ethical imperative which escapes the essentialist categorizing of humans, but it is also, so it seems, the result of what Foucauldians would call bio-political and bio-economic processes, which associate infinite individualizations with social control, therefore at least the possibility of some radical exclusions. (2005: 28)

The concept of race continues to function as a transcendent politics that can be 'infinitely' signified in relation to – and *for* – radical exclusions. Balibar (2005) suggested that there is a differentiation that is used to create a 'hierarchic totality' – such as racial typologies – and a differentiation that is premised on the relationship of difference to singularities (that is, *difference-in-itself*). Balibar (2005: 26) contended:

> how identities always 'differ from themselves', or the fact that the most fundamental difference, the one that precisely resists the classifications and typologies, or its own fixation as essential difference, always arises from oneself or to be absolutely *different* is also, indeed to differ from

any difference that has been ascribed to the singular by narratives of domination and objectification.

Race and racism, therefore, continue to maintain particular (unequal) social orders even if the kinds of possibilities ushered forth by *difference-in-itself* signal an alternative, new and 'dangerous' politics – a politics that directly challenges the assumptions of Taylor's multiculturalism and metaphysical realism with contemporary instances of neoliberal multiculturalism and ontological pluralism. It may have something more to do with what Grosz (2002: 468) suggests when she asks: 'Can we reconceive politics without identity?'

Reflections

We are acutely, painfully, aware that the preceding discussion on difference-in-itself and the limits of identity, that include claims about 'intensive multiplicities', 'plural ontologies' and 'neoliberal multiculturalism', can be read as evidence of our privileged racial positions as part of White supremacy in the academy. Further, we know that such claims mark us in ways that denote how we lie outside of the racisms that people in this research face every day.

Our discussion about a 'creolization' of humans does nothing to stop those who advocate demeaning, injurious and eugenic practices based on ideas of racial identities. Moreover, our worries about 'cultural absolutists' will likely be read as a kind of complicity with White supremacy that prevents genuine attempts to rectify racial exclusions from the benefits afforded others by representative governments. In other words, it is not very clear how rethinking ontological conditions produces an alternative politics that eradicates racisms, nor what can be the ontological basis for ethics (Rekret, 2016).

We are not sure ourselves. This admission will likely be seen as a failure of the concepts we employ, or even of us as academics, rather than to do with the relative intractability of the historical practices of racism and racial exclusions. Nevertheless, we can say with a high degree of certainty that most recognitive attempts at racial equity in education are *already* coopted through neoliberal multiculturalism, and hence retain the arrangements of White hegemony.

And we can say, further, with a high degree of certainty, that using school-choice policies as forms of racial equity perpetuate capitalist arrangements that are indeed *not* free (that is, 'free markets') but entirely dependent on power arrangements that code for racialised exclusions and that now commodify racialised identities.

Our focus on the ontological provides our analysis with ways to understand how contemporary democratic practices are swallowed up by economic conditions. The emphasis on the ontological provides an interruption to these commodifying properties; an interruption that affords others opportunities to engage in politics that are not dictated by us or other academics.

Albeit dangerous, these interruptions reorient political attention towards the very structures that pattern and condition politics. A critique of neoliberal education must confront the very ideas of representation, recognition and difference that its liberal predecessors depend on to arrange the exclusion of others. Educational equity will likely not occur through the 'improvement of schools', but by interrupting the instruments, mechanisms and technologies that support, legitimate and circulate logics of liberal representation and difference in order to perpetuate capitalist education practices.

SIX

Policy events, race and the future of the city

> It was all about how do you meet the needs of the students and their families? And it wasn't that an Africentric school was the answer. It was that there wasn't one answer. (Black Canadian, Trustee, TDSB)

This book has worked from the premise that policy is ad hoc and uncertain, and that one way to undertake policy analysis is through a policy problematisation that would 'identify conditions and registers that have disqualified parallel (that is, rival, contradictory) thoughts, practices, and enactments' (Webb and Gulson, 2015a: 40). We have explored the multiple ways in which the policy event of the Africentric Alternative School could be traced and mapped, to speak to the idea that there was no one answer either to Black schooling in Toronto or to why and how the school was established. Our policy problematisation has identified several effects of the policy event (the development of the Africentric Alternative School) that do not have clear outcomes or hidden truths.

In each chapter we have been interested in the idea that policy events have no determinate outcomes – and no determinate origins – which reproduce events due to the role that chance has in our evental lives. As we outlined in the introductory chapter, we have been interested in the idea of an abductive approach, as 'concerned with the relationship between a situation and inquiry' (Brinkmann, 2014: 722), that meant – as St Pierre and Jackson noted (citing Deleuze and Guattari) – that we work 'through the middle' without a beginning or end to analysis (St Pierre and Jackson, 2014). In these final thoughts of this book, we realise we have, perhaps, been undertaking work not just 'through the middle' but that we have attempted to undertake what Deleuze called looking at 'in between', and that this sums up our interest in refusing one or even multiple 'origins' linked to narrative expositions about the Africentric Alternative School. Deleuze, in reflecting on contemporary thought, stated:

> If things aren't going too well in contemporary thought,
> it's because there's a return under the name of 'modernism'
> to abstractions, back to the problem of origins, all that
> sort of thing ... It was no longer a question of starting
> or finishing. The question was rather, what happens 'in
> between'? (Deleuze, 1990a: 121)

Deleuze combined philosophy and thought with 'physical movement'
and sports like surfing. He proposes that:

> There's no longer an origin as starting point, but a sort of
> putting-into-orbit. The key thing is how to get taken up
> in the motion of a big wave, a column of rising air, to 'get
> into something' instead of being the origin of an effort.
> (Deleuze, 1990b: 121)

This is a book, therefore, about a policy event that we approached
in the sense of 'getting into something' that certainly was already in
motion. Hence the chapters are attempts, like surfing, to ride what is in
front of it, but also aware, upon reflection, that the wave is made up of
disparate series of events, composed by any number of in/compossibles
distributed unequally across time and space. We would suggest this is
what we have tried to do. We know that the lack of 'chronology' in the
chapters, and the separation of the middle chapters into two separate
texts, may have been unsettling – or downright annoying – though we
hope that this has been compensated by our descriptions and analyses
of different events.

   In each chapter we have attempted to show how a seemingly disparate
series of events is able to be marshalled into specific and multiple
narratives about the establishment of the Africentric Alternative School
– violence, anti-racism and race-based statistics, policy entrepreneurs,
the rebirth of alternative schools as a neoliberal choice mechanism. Yet,
as the chapter structure was intended to enunciate, both within each
chapter and across them, what we have posited as the incompossibility
of education policy indicates that when education policy appears
to produce a clear outcome, such as the physical establishment
of the Africentric school, it can be constituted by contradiction,
incompleteness and indeterminancy (for example, Ball, 1994). As we
hope to have shown, there is a sense in which the policy event of the
establishment of the school has no beginning and no end, and yet,
nonetheless, can still manifest as a crucial intervention in education
policy in the city.

School choice and living in desperate times

> First of all you get a perspective from basically, with all due respect white guys, that have never grown up in the projects or understand the problems. I think many of them mean well, but there's a difference between meaning well and understanding that we live in desperate times. And in desperate times, you take desperate measures, nothing else is working. (Weiss, 2010: Film time 16.16–16.44)

The utilisation of the alternative schools programme, now framed as a choice policy, to establish a Black-focused school in Toronto, can be considered, as we have noted, as a 'politics *of no longer waiting*'. We contend that for Black community members, parents and students this is similar to the ways in which African American support for choice has often been about choice within public systems. Scott (2012), citing Pedroni (2007), posited that this is a form of 'strategic engagement' where school choice, especially charter schools, becomes a site of political engagement that enables Black parents to circumvent conditions of underfunded and demonised comprehensive public schools, and limited educational options (Scott, 2012: 193).

What we can see here is the ways that, problematically, markets are mobilised as equity moves, which deliberately obscures, if not overtly eschews, principles of fairness: 'The racial politics of educational advocacy defy easy characterizations ... Communities of color and progressive reformers have sought to participate in market reforms to escape undesirable schooling options within the traditional public system' (Scott, 2011: 582).

Toronto is a reflection of broader global trends towards the use of market reforms to create state-funded, 'safe' spaces such as Islamic schools (Gulson and Webb, 2013). In the United States, Scott notes that market reforms make progressive politics problematic, especially when pernicious and retrograde ideas have been introduced into public systems. For example: 'At times, this has meant that the market options are comparatively more progressive than some regressive state or school district policies' (Scott, 2011: 582), and choice is posited as a civil rights issue (Scott, 2013).

In the US, advocacy of choice has come from conservative philanthropies and think tanks. This is less the case in Canada and in Toronto, though free market think tanks, most notably the Fraser Institute, have long lent their support to the introduction of choice more broadly, and have advocated for the introduction of charter schools across provinces. Hence, it is clear to us that ideology is, at the very least, a malleable and undependable heuristic for political analyses of Black-focused schooling in Toronto. At its worst, ideology promises political mobilisations that simply never occur and rarely, if ever, benefit those who have been racialised under its seduction. If ideological imaginings do provide respite, it is through the registers of markets that distribute economised choices of difference and representation.

What this complicated politics does speak to is the relationship between policy and race where Black students have been problems to 'fix' or 'correct'. Dumas et al inverted this idea, contending that:

> although much educational policy research situates communities of color as on the receiving end of policy interventions, as the 'object' of policy, or, the 'problem' to be fixed by policy, a cultural politics of race invites, even insists on, turning that configuration on its head. (Dumas et al, 2016: 4)

Market logics, therefore, open up uncomfortable spaces about choice and Black politics. Spence (2012) proposed the notion of Black governmentality, where neoliberalism is not only something that acts upon Black communities, but 'this dynamic is reproduced within, and not simply on black communities' (Spence, 2012: 140). In Toronto, the use of race-based statistics and the establishing of the Africentric school within a framework of existing policies, was similar to Spence's contention that 'a range of problems within black communities have been taken outside the realm of the political by rendering them *technical* and *actionable*' (Spence, 2012: 140). Moreover, culture is made part of these actions but it cannot be seen as outside of economised and technical solutions. The situation becomes one where there are no ideological commitments outside of neoliberalisation, certainly not 'progressive' ones, for, as Brown (2015) notes, neoliberalism has recast, that is, refuses, the possibility of any idealised forms of democratic politics.

We might see that, in Toronto, what the establishment of the Africentric Alternative School demonstrated is a similar debate to that on educational choice for Black families in the United States; that 'Black families hold a "bracketed freedom" in choosing alternative schooling for their children unless they can access larger power sources to rise above the racial politics inherent in U.S. public and private education' (Stevenson et al, 2012: 270). We know that the idea of a small school rectifying the historical and contemporary conditions for Black students is unlikely. Nonetheless, in Toronto, there is now a 'Black-focused' school where there was none. Even if the school is closed at some time in the future, it cannot be erased from the landscape of schooling history – it has set precedent for the next radicalised and/or educational event.

The school was seen as a spatial intervention – one that could contribute to and repudiate the racialisation of urban space. The establishment of the school, furthermore, has reshaped what is possible as racial politics in the city, and how culture is connected to race in Toronto. Hence, when the school was being proposed, the idea of an Afrocentric education was subject not just to debates about what is Black, but also debates about the ways that culture entered the neoliberal multicultural framing, where culture is racialised, and anti-racist politics becomes neoliberalised.

Where did racism go? Culture and anti-racism in the education market

> We can only deal with racism if we critically interrogate race and racial differences and what these mean. If we reclaim the idea that race is about identity and politics, it offers new possibilities in working to resist oppression. It may otherwise be simply wished away or placed in a closet, as if by not speaking about it we have peace and harmony. For most racially oppressed bodies, race is always the big elephant in the classroom space. We cannot simply address racism by remaining silent. Education must affirm that race is about Black, Asian, Indigenous and White people. These identities evoke different responses, punishment for some, and for some, privilege and power. Education should teach about the social construction of racial identities and how they are systemically paired with rewards and punishment. Notwithstanding good intentions, we have a bankrupt educational system. (Dei, 2013: 124)

We could follow Dei here, and propose that (a) schooling in neoliberal societies is White supremacy (Leonardo, 2009); (b) neoliberal education policy, even despite, or perhaps due to, 'good intentions', is similarly White supremacy (Gillborn, 2005); and (c) now racialised and economised subjects enact White supremacy desires (rather than, or in concert with, White supremacy desires – that is, the erasure or 'obscurification' of the state (Goldberg, 2009; Gulson and Webb, 2013).

While we would be happy to hold these positions, in this book we have also been interested in the limits of identity, including identity as the premise for anti-racism or as part of liberal and neoliberal multiculturalism. We have been interested in how the specificity of identity has been used to mobilise collective action around schooling, while occurring within a marketised policy environment.

The establishment of the Africentric Alternative School denoted the ways in which race and culture work materially and representationally. In its establishment, the school became a physical place in a part of the multicultural city. Hence, being a Black-focused school in a multicultural city entered the fraught terrain of what particular identity would be intelligible. The establishment of the school and the contestation over difference and Black identity indicated the ways in which, like all identities, it may be futile to make:

> any attempt to homogenize and articulate a singular Black identity and commonplace blackness, especially one tied to a particular nation. In addressing this reality, Walcott (2003) offers an alternative to conceptualizing blackness in Canada. In *Black Like Who?*, he writes of the need to acknowledge the variety of 'blacknesses' in Canada and how diaspora sensibilities are more fruitful in understanding the realities of lived blackness ... Thus, such sensibilities offer spaces for the meaningful inclusion of blacknesses in cultural dialogue. (Neverson, 2014: 1854)

It was in these spaces that the Africentric school constituted, and was constituted by, a public discussion about the relationship between race and culture. In the school's representation as an ethical decision – that is, a necessary response to violence, to educational disadvantage and to racism – the school complicated the political debate about difference in Toronto. The school forced questions about when 'markers of race, ethnicity and cultural difference are rendered speakable, visible and recognisable as categories marked with *specific* ethical values' (Keith, 2005: 18).

What became clear about the school was that, whereas the collecting of race-based statistics became normalised, the idea that these statistics would create a momentum to establish a Black-focused curriculum and Black-focused schooling was one step too far. A school could only be cultural not racial in self-identification – hence Africentric, not Black. The problem was the school was entering a school market as fixed or unchangeable. As Lentin and Titley note: 'Cultural attributes, just as much as physical ones, can come to be associated with particular groups of people, interpreted as fixed and unchangeable, effecting a racialization put to justificatory work in and through hierarchies and structures of power' (Lentin and Titley, 2011: 63).

We think, therefore, that the Africentric Alternative School posed a question for policy and for racial politics. Goldberg posits one that we might ask for the future of cultural institutions like schooling in cities, when identity continues to be the demarcation and posited solution to difference. And yet, identity resonates, is redolent, is required, in the marketised education systems where identity has become the marker. As Gilroy noted:

> Identity has ... been taken into the viscera of postmodern commerce, where the goal of planetary marketing promotes not just the targeting of objects and services to the identities of particular consumers but the idea that any product whatsoever can be suffused with identity. Any commodity is open to being 'branded' in ways that solicit identification and try to orchestrate identity. (Gilroy, 2000: 98)

This is part of the debates that we see about whether school choice is segregating, on whether policy should support separation; and, in either case, a debate that is accelerated within market forms of governance, that by necessity, require segmentations – that is, market niches – to operate. In the end, the debate about separation or segregation is a kind of ersatz or 'empty' politics that only reflects the contemporary economic organisation of life through brands and competition. While in Toronto the debate over segregation and separation evoked a stark history of power, the market exploits these historical contradictions in ways that equivocate imaginations of equality, equity and liberal democracy.

The policy event of the school demonstrated how commodification in the city depoliticises difference. We contend that it is crucial to understand the connection of the city to education policy, not only as education reshapes the city, but that the city is an articulation of racial politics. Keith asserts that:

> it is ... the categoric instability of the boundaries of ethnicity and the subjects of racialisation that renders the spaces of the city singularly significant in the articulation of both identity mimesis and political mobilisation. The city does not merely mediate such relations, it becomes

simultaneously both polis and area of communication.
(Keith, 2005: 180)

This idea of mimesis, of representation, holds for the ways in which the Africentric school is an articulation of commodified difference in the city. The Africentric school used an alternative school framework but could not be alternative (because it was not White). This illustrates the naïve idea that choice is always neutral, except, of course, when Black people are choosing, and the concomitant naïveté that policy is the mediator of, and not producer of, racism. Hence, ethnicity's mimesis instructs education policy to be simultaneously a contradiction in materiality – that is education policy is both an instrument of equality *and* racism. The mobilisation of this device, through choice frameworks, re-territorialises the city within racial contradictions.

Arguments about whether the Africentric school was a safe place, a separated place, and so forth, were also about how difference was managed in the city. The discussion was about whether it was legitimate even to attempt to frame the school as a political move, rather than to do with choice (and hence neutral). It converged with other forms of representation that were about both recognising race and occluding it into culture. As a form of depoliticisation, one tracing here sees that the school emerges or is recognised in market mechanics.

> Depoliticization involves removing a political phenomenon from comprehension of its *historical* emergence and from a recognition of the *powers* that produce and contour it. No matter its particular form and mechanics, depoliticization always eschews power and history in the representation of its subject. (Brown, 2006: 15)

As we noted in Chapter Five, race has become privatised but racism remains a key component of neoliberalism (Goldberg, 2009). Spence argues that anti-racism has become a 'public principle' but a neoliberalised principle. For example, educational neoliberalism subverted, indeed economised, a collective response to racism, and instead created a market for different identities to compete. Neoliberal education policy is both an opportunity for those committed to anti-racism and a problem when the commodification of culture risks reducing people to different discourses of property. Hence, while anti-racism may be a public principle, 'under neoliberalism the most effective means of combatting racism are developing entrepreneurial capacities in populations, institutions, and spaces deemed as "non-white"" (Spence, 2012: 145).

Racial biopolitics or the post-racial? The Africentric Alternative School as the future of the city

> [The Africentric Alternative School is an example of] typical weathervanes of public opinion around issues of multiculturalism, religion, immigration and 'race'. Ideas of universalism and cultural relativism are prominent in this debate in which identity politics dominates the discourse. As has been the case in previous such public conversations, the culturalization of difference is the prime default option for all involved. As policies are to be found for protracted urban problems, categorizations along ethnic lines are easier to come by than complex social problems. (Boudreau et al, 2009: 97–8)

Boudreau et al (2009) posit that the Africentric Alternative School could portend resegregation in the city of Toronto. This epigraph is yet another example of the way that one small school within a school became a marker for the possible future of the city. While this may seem a ludicrous proposition, we suggest, as we did at the beginning of this book, that the singular story, and singular stories, of the Africentric Alternative School tell us something more general about education policy and the city. To repeat the point we made, we are interested in the story of the school and a broad idea of generalisability – that is, 'how the singular becomes delaminated from its location in someone's story or some locale's irreducibly local history and circulated as evidence of something shared' (Berlant, 2011: 12). Across the course of this book, we have been hoping to be able to map 'the becoming general of singular things' (Berlant, 2011: 12).

We contend that what the policy event of the Africentric Alternative School indicates is not policy on the one hand and racial biopolitics on the other. Policy is a form of racial biopolitics, and race is now produced through neoliberal markets, in conjunction with earlier liberal categories. This leads to questions such as 'What does race do? How does race function?' (Swanton, 2008: 2338), as much as to asking how we know race and questioning the limits of anti-racism in markets. Johnson (2013) proposed, in reference to the Africentric school:

> Based on Toronto's legacy of district equity policies, many White residents continue to view their local public schools as inclusive and characterized the recent Africentric school proposal as separatist and divisive. Some Black community activists, on the other hand, contend that these progressive policy changes in the Toronto school system over time have been largely 'cosmetic' and have not substantially altered the career paths or life chances of African Canadian students. While publicly supporting the Africentric Alternative School as a vehicle for educational change, they continue to pursue community-based educational strategies and programs. (2013: 16)

As we have noted in this book, at various times community-based educational strategies and programmes have been pursued to attempt to redress Black student disadvantage, including supporting the development of pilot curriculum initiatives. Additionally, race-based statistics, while a form of 'counting' and/or measuring that is a preferred neoliberal tactic in the economisation and marketisation of schooling, had been pushed in order to highlight the absence of race in the violence against Black residents, and disadvantage of Black students, in Toronto. The establishment of the Africentric school through the alternative school policy, occurring after the normalisation of choice in Canadian schooling, conceivably entered a realm where choice presumes that all options are equal. That is, to repeat Brown (2015), governance through the management of rules rather than other principles for dealing with difference.

In the case of the Africentric Alternative School, race is operationalised through policy, and is part of technologies of governance or management, following Brown (2015). Neoliberalism induces people to be policy entrepreneurs who live, and enact, racial biopolitics, not the state. This positions policy entrepreneurs to simultaneously reject and accept the (liberal) histories of racial biopolitics in relation to new forms of racial biopolitics, where people are induced to feel empowered through the market. This can mean creating a 'culture-specific school' based on biological aggregates and phenotype grouping, and accounted for through acts of violence, Othering, counting and categorisations. Particular forms of rationalities are used by people to govern themselves through varied practices, in association with corresponding and contradictory logics or rationales for race – 'raciologies' – and school markets.

However, what was clear was that a small school within a school created a fissure in the comfortable reading of difference in the city. Violence against Black residents and endemic Black disadvantage was not considered a crisis, or simply ignored despite being the focus of much political activity in the mid-1990s and mid-2000s. However, the establishment of a school that would be identified as Black was enough to create a massive national disruption. The school circulated in a city where difference is not internal but continues to be captured by recognition – particularly when this recognition is marketised and commodified. The Black phenotype becomes attributed to a place, a spatial fetishisation, hence the school becomes a body. As Amin notes in reference to the persistence of racial biopolitics, and as we noted in in Chapter Five, there has been a return, a rise, of the phenotype, and the ways in which the body as racial marker acts as a trigger (and precisely how Deleuze [2006] discussed the way the prehensions of an event orient the body). This work, as Amin posits, 'refers to an everyday but poorly understood practice of racial coding with deep historical and biological roots, recursively sensing some bodies to be inferior, discrepant and threatening' (2010: 4).

That is, even the insults about the school, even the violence against Black students, even the idea of Black failure, these all remain part of what Goldberg calls 'neoliberalism's postracial condition'. Post-racial, that is, not in the sense that racism was eradicated, but rather that what can occur is the 'employ[ing of] these various instrumentalizing racial animations while denying they add up to racism. Or *denying indeed that racial characterization is being invoked*' (Goldberg, 2015: 87). For Goldberg, the post-racial is what enables particular forms of denial, in that 'neoliberal postraciality amounts to 'racisms without racism' (Goldberg, 2015: 81–2).

However, against this backdrop, Goldberg asks: what if an identity, even a racialised one, was given up? And this is, we think, a pertinent question to ask in reference to the Africentric Alternative School: 'How might a society configure itself outside the bounds of the racial while mindful of its debilitating racist histories? And how might people live their lives relationally unrestricted by racial convention and contention, by racisms?' (Goldberg, 2015: 170). Leonardo similarly contends that this is a difficult but necessary question: 'But it is important to consider the implications of post-race in order to continually re-examine long-held beliefs about race and whether the ultimate existential choice of disappearing is warranted in order to reappear as something else we would prefer' (Leonardo, 2013: 154).

We suggest that the policy event of the Africentric Alternative School may force us either to accept the continuation of racial biopolitics and the maintenance of phenotypical racism, or it might force us to debate about what a post-racial city might look like. We would argue that the policy event of the Africentric school can help us to understand our capacity to imagine new futures for policy, for schools and the city.

References

AAS (Africentric Alternative School) (2011) Africentric Alternative School 2011, 30 May. Retrieved from: http://schoolweb.tdsb.on.ca/africentricschool/Home.aspx

African Canadian Legal Clinic (2008) Disaggregated data collection (race-based statistics). Policy paper. Retrieved from: www.aclc.net/wp-content/uploads/Policy-Papers-1-11-English-FINAL.pdf

Allen, J. (2003) *Lost geographies of power*, Oxford: Blackwell

Amin, A. (2010) The remainders of race, *Theory, Culture & Society*, *27*, 1, 1–23

Amin, A. and Thrift, N. (2002) *Cities: Reimagining the urban*, Cambridge: Polity Press

Anderson, B. (2014) *Encountering affect: Capacities, apparatuses, conditions*, Farnham: Ashgate

Anderson, B., & Harrison, P. (2010) The promise of non-representational theories. In B. Anderson & P. Harrison (eds), *Taking-place: Non-representational theories and geography*, Farnham: Ashgate, 1-36

Anderson, S.E. and Jaafar, S.B. (2003) Policy trends in Ontario education: 1990–2003. ICEC Working Paper 1. Retrieved from: http://fcis oise utoronto ca/~icec/policytrends pdf

Anonymous (2015) Quebec considers removing N-word from 11 place names. CBC News. Retrieved from: www.cbc.ca/news/canada/ottawa/quebec-considers-removing-n-word-from-11-place-names-1.3184317

Aveling, N. (2009) Rebranding Jane and Finch, *The Star*, 8 January. Retrieved from: https://www thestar com/news/gta/2009/01/08/rebrand ing_jane_and _finch html

Bacchi, C. (2000) Policy as discourse: What does it mean? Where does it get us?, *Discourse: Studies in the Cultural Politics of Education*, *21*, 1, 45–57

Bacchi, C. (2012) Why study problematizations? Making politics visible, *Open Journal of Political Science*, *2*, 1–8

Baker, B. (2002) The hunt for disability: The new eugenics and the normalization of school children, *Teachers College Record*, *104*, 4, 663–703

Balibar, E. (2005) Difference, otherness, exclusion, *parallax*, *11*, 1, 19–34

Ball, S.J. (1994) *Education reform: A critical and post-structural approach*, Philadelphia, PA: Open University Press

Ball, S.J. (2008) *The education debate*, Bristol: Policy Press

Ball, S.J. (2013) *Foucault, power and education*, New York: Routledge

Ball, S.J., Maguire, M. and Braun, A. (2012) *How schools do policy: Policy enactments in secondary schools*, London: Routledge

Begin, M., Caplan, G., Bhartu, M., Glaze, A., Murphy, D., and Di Cecco, R. (1994) For the love of learning: Report of the royal commission on learning. Retrieved from: https://archive.org/details/forloveoflearnin04onta

Berlant, L.G. (2011) *Cruel optimism*, Durham, NC: Duke University Press

Bonnett, A. and Carrington, B. (2000) Fitting into categories or falling between them? Rethinking ethnic classification, *British Journal of Sociology of Education*, *21*, 4, 487–500

Boudreau, J., Keil, R. and Young, D. (2009) *Changing Toronto: Governing urban neoliberalism*, Toronto: University of Toronto Press

Brennan, R. and Brown, L. (2005) Premier rejects black schools, *Toronto Star*, 15 September, B01

Brinkmann, S. (2014) Doing without data, *Qualitative Inquiry*, *20*, 6, 720–25

Brown, L. (2005a) Educator calls for creation of Black schools, *Toronto Star*, 3 February, np

Brown, L. (2005b) Black-only school proposed, *Toronto Star*, 14 September, A01

Brown, L. (2008a) Black school site is picked, *Toronto Star*, 26 April. Retrieved from: www.thestar.com/life/parent/2008/04/26/black_school_site_is_picked html

Brown, L. (2008b) Sheppard school parents okay Africentric program, *Toronto Star*, 2 May. Retrieved from: www.thestar.com/news/gta/2008/05/02/sheppard_school_parents_okay_africentric_program html

Brown, L. (2008c) Parents welcome Africentric school, *Toronto Star*, 3 May. Retrieved from: www.thestar.com/news/gta/2008/05/03/parents_welcome_africentric_school html

Brown, W. (2006) *Regulating aversion: Tolerance in the age of identity and empire*, Princeton, NJ: Princeton University Press

Brown, W. (2015) *Undoing the demos: Neoliberalism's stealth revolution*, Brooklyn, NY: Zone Books.

Buzzelli, M. (2001) From little Britain to Little Italy: An urban ethnic landscape study in Toronto, *Journal of Historical Geography*, *27*, 4, 573–87

Chubb, J. and Moe, T. (1988) Politics, markets and the organization of schools, *American Political Science Review*, *82*, 1065–89

Chubb, J. and Moe, T. (1990) *Politics, markets and America's schools*, Washington, DC: Brookings Institution

Chung, A. (2005) A call for 'separateness', *Toronto Star*, 8 October, A01

Clough, P.T. and Willse, C. (2011) Human security/national security: gender branding and population racism. In P.T. Clough and C. Willse (eds), *Beyond biopolitics: Essays on the goverance of life and death*, Durham, NC: Duke University Press, 46–64

Collins, J. (2000) The other Sydney: Cultural and social diversity in Western Sydney. In J. Collins and S. Poynting (eds), *The other Sydney: Communities, identities and inequalities in Western Sydney*, Melbourne: Common Ground Publishing, 34–60

Comaroff, J.L. and Comaroff, J. (2009) *Ethnicity, Inc.*, Chicago: University of Chicago Press

Danius, S., Jonsson, S., and Spivak, G. C. (1993) An interview with Gayatri Chakravorty Spivak, *Boundary*, 20, 2, 24-50.

Davies, B.D. and Bansel, P. (2007) Neoliberalism and education, *International Journal of Qualitative Studies in Education*, 20, 3, 247–59

Davies, S. (2004) School choice by default? Understanding the demand for private tutoring in Canada, *American Journal of Education*, *110*, 3, 233–55

Dei, G.J.S. (1995) Examining the case for 'African-centred' schools in Ontario, *McGill Journal of Education*, *30*, 2, 179–98

Dei, G.J.S. (1996) The role of Afrocentricity in the inclusive curriculum in Canadian schools, *Canadian Journal of Education*, *21*, 2, 170–86

Dei, G.J.S. (2005) The case for Black school, *Toronto Star*, 4 February, A19

Dei, G.J.S. (2008) Schooling as community: Race, schooling, and the education of African youth, *Journal of Black Studies, 38,* 3, 346–66

Dei, G.J.S. (2013) Africentric schooling: What next? *International Journal for Talent Development and Creativity*, *1*, 2, 119–28

Dei, G.J.S. and Kempf, A. (2005) The application and impact of race-based statistics to effect systemic change and eliminate institutional racism. Paper presented at the Canadian Race-Relations Foundation Policy Dialogue, 21 October, Toronto

Dei, G.J.S. and Kempf, A. (2013) *New perspectives on African-centred education in Canada*, Toronto: Canadian Scholars' Press

Deleuze, G. (1990a) *The logic of sense*, trans. M. Lester and C. Stivale, edited by C.V. Boundas, New York: Columbia University Press

Deleuze, G. (1990b) *Mediators Negotiations, 1972–1990*, New York: Columbia University Press

Deleuze, G. (1991) *Bergsonism*, trans. H. Tomlinson and B. Habberjam, New York: Zone Books

Deleuze, G. (1993) What is an event? In *The fold: Leibniz and the Baroque*, New York: Continuum

Deleuze, G. (1994) *Difference and repetition*, New York: Continuum International Publishing Group

Deleuze, G. (2006) What is an event? In *The fold: Leibniz and the Baroque*, New York, NY: Continuum, 86–93

Deleuze, G. and Guattari, F. (1987 [1980]) *A thousand plateaus: Capitalism and schizophrenia*, Minneapolis: University of Minnesota Press

Delhi, K. (1996) Travelling tales: Education reform and parental 'choice' in postmodern times, *Journal of Education Policy*, *11*, 1, 75–88

Diebel, L. (2008) Family fuelled the fight, *Toronto Star*, 31 January, A6

Dippo, D. and James, C.E. (2011) The urbanization of suburbia: Implications for inner-suburban schools and communities. In D. Young, P.K. Wood and R. Keil (eds), *In-between infrastructure [electronic resource]: Urban connectivity in an age of vulnerability*, Kelowna, BC: Praxis e Press, 115–30

Dumas, M.J., Dixson, A.D. and Mayorga, E. (2016) Educational policy and the cultural politics of race: Introduction to the special issue, *Educational Policy*, *30*, 1, 3–12

Dwyer, C. and Bressey, C. (eds) (2008) *New geographies of race and racism*, Aldershot: Ashgate

East York Mirror (2008) Possible Africentric school sites to be chosen this month, 10 April. Retrieved from: www insidetoronto com/news-story/20734-possible-africentric-school-sites-to-be-chosen-this-month/

Easton, D. (1953) *The political system*, New York: Knopf

Edwards, R. (2002) Mobilizing lifelong learning: Governmentality in educational practices, *Journal of Education Policy*, *17*, 3, 353–65

Foucault, M. (1977) *Discipline and punish: The birth of the prison*, New York: Vintage/Random House

Foucault, M. (1982) *The archeology of knowledge*, New York: Pantheon

Foucault, M. (2000) Questions of method. In J.D. Faubion (ed.), *Michel Foucault: Power, essential works of Foucault 1954–1984*, vol. 3, London: Penguin, 223–38

Foucault, M. (2003) *Society must be defended: Lectures at the Collège de France, 1975–1976*, New York: Picador

Foucault, M. (2008) *The birth of biopolitics: Lectures at the Collège de France, 1978–1979*, New York: Palgrave Macmillan

Fraser, N. (1995) From redistribution to recognition: Dilemmas of justice in a 'post-socialist' age, *New Left Review*, 212, July-August, 68-93

Fraser, N. (2009) Feminism, capitalism and the cunning of history, *New Left Review*, 56, 97–117

Friedman, M. (1962) *Capitalism and freedom*, Chicago, IL: University of Chicago Press

Friedman, M. (1980) *Free to choose*, New York: Harcourt Brace Jovanovich

Gerrard, J. (2013) Self-help and protest: The emergence of black supplementary schooling in England, *Race Ethnicity and Education*, 16, 1, 32–58

Gidney, R.D. (1999) *From Hope to Harris: The reshaping of Ontario's schools*, Toronto: University of Toronto Press

Gillborn, D. (2005) Education policy as an act of white supremacy: Whiteness, critical race theory and education reform, *Journal of Education Policy*, 20, 4, 485–505

Gillborn, D. (2010) The colour of numbers: Surveys, statistics and deficit thinking about race and class, *Journal of Education Policy*, 25, 2, 251–74

Gilroy, P. (2000) *Against race: Imagining political culture beyond the color line*, Cambridge, MA: Harvard University Press

Glissant, É. (1989) *Caribbean discourse*, trans. M. Dash, Charlottesville: University of Virginia Press

Goldberg, D.T. (2009) *The threat of race: Reflections of racial neoliberalism*, Malden, MA: Blackwell

Goldberg, D.T. (2015) *Are we all postracial yet?* Cambridge: Polity Press

Goonewardena, K. and Kipfer, S. (2005) Spaces of difference: Reflections from Toronto on multiculturalism, bourgeois urbanism and the possibility of radical urban politics, *International Journal of Urban and Regional Research*, 29, 3, 670–8

Gregory, D. (2004) *The colonial present*, Oxford: Blackwell

Grosz, E. (2002) A politics of imperceptibility: A response to 'Anti-racism, multiculturalism, and the ethics of identification', *Philosophy and Social Criticism*, 28, 4, 463–72

Gulson, K.N. (2011) *Education policy, space and the city: Markets and the in visibility of race*, New York: Routledge

Gulson, K.N. and Webb, P.T. (2013) 'We had to hide we're Muslim': Ambient fear, Islamic schools and the geographies of race and religion, *Discourse: Studies in the Cultural Politics of Education*, 34, 4, 628–41

Hacking, I. (2005) Why race still matters, *Daedalus*, 134, 1, 102–16

Hacking, I. (2016) Biopower and the avalanche of printed numbers. In V.W. Cisney and N. Morar (eds), *Biopower: Foucault and beyond*, Chicago: University of Chicago Press, 65–81

Hackworth, J. (2007) *The neoliberal city: Governance, ideology, and development in American urbanism*, Ithaca, NY: Cornell University Press

Hackworth, J. and Rekers, J. (2005) Ethnic packaging and gentrification: The case of four neighbourhoods in Toronto, *Urban Affairs Review, 41*, 2, 211–36

Hage, G. (1998) *White nation: Fantasies of white supremacy in a muticultural nation*, Sydney: Pluto Press

Hale, C.R. (2005) Neoliberal multiculturalism: The remaking of cultural rights and racial dominance in Central America, *PoLAR: Political and Legal Anthropology Review, 28*, 1, 10–28

Harney, S. and Moten, F. (2013) *The undercommons: Fugitive planning and black study*, Brooklyn: Minor Compositions

Heimans, S. (2012) Coming to matter in practice: Enacting education policy, *Discourse: Studies in the Cultural Politics of Education, 33*, 2, 313–26

Henry, F. and Tator, C. (2005) *Racial profiling in Toronto: Discourses of domination, mediation, and opposition*, Toronto: Canadian Race Relations Foundation

Hubbard, P. (2006) *City*, London: Routledge

Hulchanski, J.D. (2010) *The three cities within Toronto: Income polarization among Toronto's neighbourhoods, 1970–2005*, Toronto: Cities Centre, University of Toronto

James, C.E. (2011) Multicultural education in a color-blind society. In C.A. Grant and A. Portera (eds), *Intercultural and multicultural education: Enhancing global connectedness*, New York: Routledge, 191–210

James, C.E., Howard, P., Samaroo, J., Brown, R. and Parekh, G. (2015) *Africentric Alternative School research report*, Toronto: York's Centre for Education and Community/ Toronto District School Board

Johnson, L. (2013) Segregation or 'thinking Black'? Community activism and the development of Black-focused schools in Toronto and London, 1968–2008, *Teachers College Record, 115*, 1, 1–25

Kalinowski, T, and Brown, L. (2005) Province rules out black only schools, *Toronto Star*, 4 February, A01

Keith, M. (2005) *After the cosmopolitan? Multicultural cities and the future of racism*, London: Routledge

Kukutai, T. and Thompson, V. (2015) 'Inside out': The politics of enumerating the nation by ethnicity. In P. Simon, V. Piché and A.A. Gagnon (eds), *Social statistics and ethnic diversity: Cross-national perspectives in classifications and identity politics*, Dordrecht: Springer, 39–61

Kvale, S. (2006) Dominance through interviews and dialogues, *Qualitative Inquiry, 12*, 3, 480–500

Lather, P. (2006) Foucauldian scientificity: Rethinking the nexus of qualitative research and educational policy analysis, *International Journal of Qualitative Studies in Education, 19*, 6, 783–91

Lemke, T. (2011) *Biopolitics: An advanced introduction*, New York: New York University Press

Lentin, A. and Titley, G. (2011) *The crises of multiculturalism: Racism in a neoliberal age*, London: Zed Books

Leonardo, Z. (2013) *Race frameworks: A multidimensional theory of racism and education*, New York: Teachers College Press

Leonardo, Z. and Hunter, M. (2009) Imagining the urban: The politics of race, class, and schooling. In Z. Leonardo (ed.), *Race, whiteness and education*, New York: Routledge, 143–166.

Lorimer, H. (2008) Cultural geography: Non-representational conditions and concerns, *Progress in Human Geography, 32,* 4, 551–559

Levin, M. (1979) Review of 'Understanding the alternative schools movement: The retransformation of the school' by Daniel L. Luke, *Curriculum Inquiry, 9,* 4, 337–349

Lewinberg, A. (1999) Black insiders, the Black polity, and the Ontario NDP government, 1990–1995. In H. Troper and M. Weinfeld (eds), *Ethnicity, politics, and public policy: Case studies in Canadian diversity,* Toronto, ON: University of Toronto Press, 193–223

Lewis, C., Agard, R., Gopie, K. J., Harding, J., Singh, T. S., and Williams, R. (1989) The report of the race relations and policing task force. Retrieved from: https://www.siu.on.ca/pdfs/b-cover_page_letter_preface.pdf

Lewis, Stephen (1992) Report of the advisor on race relations to the premier of Ontario, Bob Rae, 9 June. Retrieved from: https://www.siu.on.ca/pdfs/report_of_the_advisor_on_race_relations_to_the_premier_of_ontario_bob_rae.pdf

Lewis Stein, D. (1993) Metro must reconsider inaction on racism study, *Toronto Star*, 9 January, A6

Lingard, B. and Rawolle, S. (2004) Mediatizing educational policy: The journalistic field, science policy, and cross-field effects, *Journal of Education Policy*, 19, 3, 361–80

Lipman, P. (2011) *The new political economy of urban education: Neoliberalism, race and the right to the city*, New York: Routledge

Lund, D.E. (1998) Social justice and public education: A response to George J. Sefa Dei, *Canadian Journal of Education, 23*, 2, 191–9

McClinchey, K.A. (2008) Urban ethnic festivals, neighborhoods, and the multiple realities of marketing place, *Journal of Travel and Tourism Marketing, 25*, 3–4, 251–64

McGaskell, T. (2005) *Race to equity: Disrupting educational inequality,* Toronto: Between the Lines

McKell, L. (2005) Transcript of comments to Black Community Education Forum – Toronto, 27 April. Retrieved from: http://action. web.ca/home/narcc/issues.shtml?x=78655

Mackey, E. (1999) *House of difference: Cultural politics and national identity in Canada,* New York: Routledge

Massey, D. (2005) *For space,* London: Sage Publications.

Miller, P. and Rose, N. (2008) *Governing the present: Administering economic, social and personal life,* Cambridge: Polity Press

Mitchell, D. (2000) *Cultural geography: A critical introduction,* Oxford: Blackwell Publishing

Mitchell, K. (2003) Educating the national citizen in neoliberal times: From the multicultural self to the strategic cosmopolitan, *Transactions of the Institute of British Geographers, 28,* 4, 387–403

Mol, A. (2002) *The body multiple: Ontology in medical practice,* Durham, NC: Duke University Press

Murdie, R. and Teixeira, C. (2011) The impact of gentrification on ethnic neighbourhoods in Toronto: A case study of Little Portugal, *Urban Studies, 48,* 1, 61–83

Murdoch, J. (2006) *Post-structuralist geography: A guide to relational space,* London: SAGE Publications

Nairin, S. (2012) The re-branding project: The genealogy of creating a neoliberal Jane and Finch, *Journal of Critical Race Inquiry, 2,* 1, 55–94

Neely, B., & Samura, M. (2011) Social geographies of race: Connecting race and space, *Ethnic and Racial Studies, 34,* 11, 1933-1952

Nelson, J.J. (2008) *Razing Africville: A geography of racism,* Toronto: University of Toronto Press

Nesbitt, N. (2013) Pre-face: Escaping race. In A. Saldanha and J.M. Adams (eds), *Deleuze and race,* Edinburgh: Edinburgh University Press

Neverson, N. (2014) The Toronto Africentric Alternative School: Media, Blackness, and discourses of multiculturalism and critical multiculturalism, *International Journal of Communication,* 8, 1851-1871

Ontario Government/African Canadian Community Working Group (1992) *Towards a new beginning: The report and action plan of the four-level government/ African Canadian Community Working Group,* Toronto

Patton, P. (1997) The world seen from within: Deleuze and the philosophy of events, *Theory and Event, 1,* 1

Pedroni, T.C. (2007) *Market movements: African American involvement in school voucher reform,* New York: Routledge

Peters, M.A. (2001) *Poststructuralism, Marxism and neoliberalism,* Oxford: Rowman and Littlefield

Petersen, E.B. (2015) What crisis of representation? Challenging the realism of post-structuralist policy research in education, *Critical Studies in Education*, *56*, 1, 147–60

Pugliese, J. (2007) Whiteness, diasporic architecture and the cultural politics of space. In S. Dasgupta (ed.), *Constellations of the transnational: Modernity, culture, critique*, Amsterdam: Rodopi, 23–49

Rabinow, P. and Rose, N. (2003) Introduction. In *The essential Foucault: Selections from essential works of Foucault 1954–1984*, New York: The New Press, vii–xxxv

Rabinow, P., & Rose, N. (2006) Biopower today, *BioSocieties, 1*, 195-217

Rankin, J. (1992) 'Black' schools split community, *Toronto Star*, 14 December, A15

Rankin, K.N. and McLean, H. (2015) Governing the commercial streets of the city: New terrains of disinvestment and gentrification in Toronto's inner suburbs, *Antipode, 47*, 1, 216–39

Rekret, P. (2016) A critique of new materialism: Ethics and ontology, *Subjectivity, 9*, 3, 225–45

Rizvi, F. and Lingard, B. (2010) *Globalizing educational policy*, London: Routledge

Robinson, A. (2007) In black or white? News Media Journalism. Retrieved from: http://apps.fims.uwo.ca/NewMedia2007/page29752618.aspx

Rofes, E. and Stulberg, L. (eds) (2004) *The emancipatory promise of charter schools: Towards a progressive politics of school choice*, Albany: State University of New York Press

Rose, N. (1999a) *Governing the soul: The shaping of the private self*, 2nd edn, New York: Free Association Books

Rose, N. (1999b) *Powers of freedom: Reframing political thought*, Cambridge: Cambridge University Press

Rushowy, K. (2008) New TDSB head lays out vision, *Toronto Star*, 7 January. Retrieved from: http://lightskyenergy com/yourtoronto/education/2008/01/07/new_tdsb_head_lays_out_vision html

Scheurich, J. (1994) Policy archaeology: A new policy studies methodology, *Journal of Education Policy, 9*, 4, 297–316

Scott, J.T. (2011) Market-driven education reform and the racial politics of advocacy, *Peabody Journal of Education, 86*, 5, 580–99

Scott, J.T. (2012) When community control meets privatization: The search for empowerment in African American Charter Schools. In D.T. Slaughter-Defoe, H.C. Stevenson, E.G. Arrington and D.J. Johnson (eds), *Black educational choice: Assessing the private and public alternatives to traditional K-12 public schools*, Santa Barbara, CA: Praeger, 173–90

Scott, J.T. (2013) A Rosa Parks moment? School choice and the marketization of civil rights, *Critical Studies in Education*, *54*, 1, 5–18

SCSAP (School Community Safety Advisory Panel) (2008) *The road to health: A final report on school safety (Falconer report)*, Toronto: Toronto District School Board

Shujaa, N.J. (1988) Parental choice of an Afrocentric independent school: Developing an explanatory theory, *Sankofa*, *2*, 1, 22–5

Shujaa, N.J. (1992) Afrocentric transformation and parental choice in African American independent schools, *Journal of Negro Education*, *61*, 2, 148–59

Simon, P. and Piché, V. (2012) Accounting for ethnic and racial diversity: The challenge of enumeration, *Ethnic and Racial Studies*, *35*, 8, 1357–65

Simons, M., Olssen, M. and Peters, M.A. (2009) Re-reading education policies, Part 1: The critical policy orientation. In M. Simons, M. Olssen and M.A. Peters (eds), *Re-reading education policies: A hand book studying the policy agenda of the 21st century*, Rotterdam: Sense Publishers, 1–35

Slaughter-Defoe, D.T., Stevenson, H.C., Arrington, E.G. and Johnson, D.J. (eds) (2012) *Black educational choice: Assessing the private and public alternatives to traditional K-12 public schools*, Denver, CO: Praeger

Soja, E. W. (1996) *Thirdspace: Journeys to Los Angeles and other real-and-imagined spaces*, Malden, MA: Blackwell

Spence, L.K. (2012) The neoliberal turn in Black politics, *Souls*, *14*, 3–4, 139–59

St Pierre, E.A. and Jackson, A.Y. (2014) Qualitative data analysis after coding, *Qualitative Inquiry*, *20*, 6, 715–19

Stagoll, C. (2010) Event. In A. Parr (ed.), *The Deleuze dictionary*, Edinburgh: Edinburgh University Press

Staunæs, D. and Pors, J.G. (2015) Thinking educational policy and management through (frictional) concepts of affect. In K.N. Gulson, M. Clarke and E.B. Petersen (eds.), *Education policy and contemporary theory: Implications for research*, London: Routledge, 99–109

Stevenson, H.C., Slaughter-Defoe, D.T., Arrington, E.G. and Johnson, D.J. (2012) Visible now? Black educational choice for the few, the desperate and the far between. In D.T. Slaughter-Defoe, H.C. Stevenson, E.G. Arrington and D.J. Johnson (eds), *Black educational choice: Assessing the private and public alternatives to traditional K-12 public schools*, Santa Barbara, CA: Praeger, 268–74

Swanton, D. (2008) Everyday multiculture and the emergence of race. In C. Dwyer and C. Bressey (eds), *New geographies of race and racism*, Aldershot: Ashgate, 239–54

Taylor, C. (1994) The politics of recognition. In A. Gutmann (ed.), *Multiculturalism: Examining the politics of recognition*, Princeton, NJ: Princeton University Press, 25–73

Taylor, C. (2009) Choice, competition, and segregation in a United Kingdom education market, *American Journal of Education, 115*, 549–68

Thompson, D. (2012) Making mixed- race: Census politics and the emergence of multiracial multiculturalism in the United States, Great Britain and Canada, *Ethnic and Racial Studies, 35*, 8, 1409–26

Thompson, D. and Wallner, J. (2011) A focusing tragedy: Public policy and the establishment of Afrocentric education in Toronto, *Canadian Journal of Political Science/Revue Canadienne de science politique, 44*, 4, 807–28

Thrift, N. (2008) *Non-representational theory: Space | politics | affect*, New York: Routledge

TDSB (Toronto District School Board) (2004a) Regular meeting, 23 June. Retrieved from: www.tdsb.on.ca/Leadership/Boardroom/AgendaMinutes.aspx?Type=M&Year=2004&Filename=40623 pdf

TDSB (2004b) Regular meeting, 20 October. Retrieved from: www.tdsb.on.ca/Leadership/Boardroom/AgendaMinutes.aspx?Type=M&Year=2004&Filename=41020 pdf

TDSB (2004c) Regular meeting, 17 November. Retrieved from: http://www.tdsb.on.ca/Leadership/Boardroom/AgendaMinutes.aspx?Type=M&Year=2004&Filename=41117.pdf

TDSB (2005a) Regular meeting, 21 September. Retrieved from: www.tdsb.on.ca/Leadership/Boardroom/AgendaMinutes.aspx?Type=M&Year=2005&Filename=50921 pdf

TDSB (2005b) Regular meeting, 14 December. Retrieved from: www.tdsb.on.ca/Leadership/Boardroom/AgendaMinutes.aspx?Type=M&Year=2005&Filename=51214 pdf

TDSB (2007a) Regular meeting, 27 June. Retrieved from: www.tdsb.on.ca/Leadership/Boardroom/AgendaMinutes.aspx?Type=M&Year=2007&Filename=70627 pdf

TDSB (2007b) *Policy P062: Alternative schools*, 27 June. Retrieved from: www2.tdsb.on.ca/ppf/uploads/files/live/91/1595.pdf

TDSB (2008) Regular meeting, 21 May. Retrieved from: http://www.tdsb.on.ca/Leadership/Boardroom/AgendaMinutes.aspx?Type=M&Year=2008&Filename=080521.pdf

TDSB (nd) Making it count: Update on the 2006 and 2008 TDSB student and parent census. Retrieved from: www.tdsb.on.ca/Portals/research/docs/reports/StudentCensusFactSheet.pdf

TDSB (2012) Alternative schools. Retrieved from: www.tdsb.on.ca/_site/ViewItem.asp?siteid=122&menuid=490&pageid=379

Wallace, A. (2009) The test: Africentric schools could be the key to success for a generation at risk. Just don't call it segregation, *This Magazine*, January–February. Retrieved from: www.thismagazine.ca/issues/2009/01/black_schools.php

Webb, P.T. (2014) Policy problematization, *International Journal of Qualitative Studies in Education*, 27, 3, 364–76

Webb, P.T. and Gulson, K.N. (2013) Policy intensions and the folds of the self, *Educational Theory*, 63, 1, 51–67

Webb, P.T. and Gulson, K.N. (2015a) *Policy, geophilosophy, education*, Rotterdam: Sense Publishers

Webb, P.T. and Gulson, K.N. (2015b) Policy scientificity 3.0: Theory and policy analysis in-and-for this world and other-worlds, *Critical Studies in Education*, 56, 1, 161–74

Weiss, A.A. (2010) *Our school* (documentary film), Canada: Aaron A. Weiss Communications: 87 minutes

Wells, A.S., Lopez, A., Scott, J. and Holme, J.J. (1999) Charter schools as postmodern paradox: Rethinking social stratification in an age of deregulated school choice, *Harvard Educational Review*, 69, 2, 172–205

Willig, R. (2012) Recognition and critique: An interview with Judith Butler, *Distinktion: Scandinavian Journal of Social Theory*, 13, 1, 139–44

Wong, J. (2011) Why educational apartheid is not the answer to curbing dropout rates for specific racial and ethnic groups, *Toronto Life*, 1 June. Retrieved from: www.torontolife.com/daily/informer/from-print-edition-informer/2011/05/31/why-educational-apartheid-is-not-the-answer-to-curbing-dropout-rates-for-specific-racial-and-ethnic-groups/

Wright, L. (1993) A year after Yonge St riot, frustrations still simmering, *Toronto Star*, 3 May, A1

Yau, M., O'Reilly, J., Rosolen, L. and Archer, B. (2011) *Census portraits: Understanding our students' ethno-racial backgrounds*, Toronto: Toronto District School Board Research & Information Services

Youdell, D. (2011) *School trouble: Identity, power and politics in education*, London: Routledge

Zine, J. (2007) Safe havens or religious 'ghettos'? Narratives of Islamic schooling in Canada, *Race, Ethnicity and Education, 10*, 1, 71–92

Index

Note: Page numbers followed by an 'n' indicate footnotes. Page numbers in *italics* refer to figures.